We are all *Differently* the *Same*

The Teachings & Insights From A Memory Of Prior Life

by Darren Hobden

Produced by:

FriesenPress
Suite 300 – 852 Fort Street
Victoria, BC, Canada V8W 1H8

www.friesenpress.com

Distributed to the trade by The Ingram Book Company

TABLE OF CONTENTS

This book is dedicated to my wife, Mette, & my children, Daniel & Anja – thank you for being such a wonderful family – love you always.

For further information about this book please visit
www.darrenhobden.com

Introduction

March 18th 1968 was a very important day for me. At around 9:20 am, I was born in a hospital in the seaside town of Eastbourne, located in the historic County of Sussex, England, and was raised in the nearby market town of Hailsham. My immediate family consisted of my mother, father and elder sister. My father worked in the construction industry, and my mother was a housewife and looked after us children. I went to both primary and secondary school, worked at different careers, socialized and raised my own family within a small radius of Hailsham until we emigrated to Vancouver Island, Canada, in 2004. I have lived here with my wife, son and daughter happily ever after.

Nothing may necessarily stand out as being different so far, but my story has a little something extra on the side. You see, ever since the day I was born, I have had a special memory. For the first few years of my life, I did not know whether I was the only person who had this memory, or whether it was something natural that we all knew about and could remember. At around eight years old, I knew that I was the only one with it, so my memory stayed a secret with me, and I never told a single person. I call it a memory and can now fully appreciate that it is a very positive and enlightening experience, but I thought no one else would understand or believe it, which is why I kept it a secret.

Fast forward around thirty-five years—I am enjoying a nice, relaxing weekend getaway with my wife, and I read a book called *The Golden Motorcycle Gang* that has similarities to my own memory, not one hundred percent the same but similar. I finished reading the book and had a good think about what the book was about. My wife and I sat down and had a discussion about the book, and at the end of the discussion, I decided to tell my memory to the first person ever—my wife.

Her reaction surprised me somewhat, for she was not only interested in my memory and found it to be quite a special experience, but she also wanted me to describe it in as much detail as I possibly could. I wrote down all the details that I could remember—I had quite a long list but could remember much more details about my memory as a child—and my wife was quite amazed by my memory and said I should voice it. I thought about this for a while and mulled it over in my mind: whether bringing my memory to the fore might benefit others. Ultimately I decided that it could in a number of ways.

I believe that my memory is a gift, given to help people who have lost loved ones and need to understand where they have gone and what they are experiencing. I believe my memory is a gift, given to help those who are either facing death or may fear dying and need to be able to accept and feel more relaxed about death. I believe that the experiences of my memory are a gift, given to the world so that people can look at things differently and that we may all get along a lot better, once we have an understanding of what my memory shows. My memory definitely shows that we are a lot more connected than some people may think. I also believe my memory is a gift, given to help us better understand that babies and young children may have a lot more spiritual knowledge than we think and that we should support that and not shut it down or suppress it.

Putting my memory into words is not necessarily an easy thing for me to do, but I truly believe that a lot of people will gain enormously through my writing of this book, and for that reason, I am willing to open up my memory to the world. If you are able to comprehend everything that I have written in this book, then that is great, and I hope you will be able to use this new insight positively in your life. Even if you take away small parts of it and are able to understand my memory, that is also great, and I hope that whatever parts you pick up will also benefit you. I would like to use this analogy: in front of you is your favourite pie, resting on a dinner plate, and you have permission to eat it all. If you can devour the whole pie, then you have enjoyed the experience and taken it for all it was worth. If you can only eat a couple of slices of pie, it has still been worthwhile, for it is a pie that you like, and having some pie is better than having no pie—besides which you can always come back for a second helping of pie whenever you feel like it. The same is true about this book.

I have written this book with the raw energy and passion that I experience when I think about my memory. I want to share it with you in this way so that you may better understand exactly what this book, and my experiences within it, is all about.

Chapter 1

Growing Up

I WANT TO GIVE YOU AN INSIGHT INTO WHO I AM. AFTER ALL, AS the old saying goes, you don't know me from Adam. What I have written in this chapter is the way that I remember it and the feelings, thoughts and experiences that went with it. I would like to share these with you to help you understand both me and my own life a little bit more.

My Early Years

My early years were quite similar to the early years of many others. As a small child, growing up in South East England in the 1970s, I went to the local playgroup and advanced on to my first day at school by attending primary school. I can remember this day as though it were yesterday and still remember entering the school and not being afraid. I went with my mum to my first class, the start of my school career. I still have this photographic memory of having a choice of two older boys I could sit next to—they would assist me in settling in at school. The boy I chose was named Michael.

At playtimes we would run around in the playground and venture into the school field to play games with other children. I even remember seeing my first dragonfly at this time and being quite amazed by it. I did not find my early school days to be daunting, in fact, I settled in straight from the off. I was actually quite enthralled by school as there were a lot of children to play with and befriend. We were, it seemed, all armed with a sense of fun, adventure and camaraderie. It reminded me a lot of my memory in some ways.

Yet one thing was different; I already knew that the memory I had inside of my young brain was unlike the memories that other people had, and so I chose not to speak of it. If I ever plucked up the courage to tell either a relative or friend about my memory, I soon pressed the eject button and decided against doing so. It was a confusing time for me, for I knew that what I had experienced—my memory— could benefit those around me. I watched the news, appalled at some of the news stories being shown; I listened to people talk about other people in a derogatory way; I witnessed bullying first hand, and I saw a lot of human behaviour going on that shocked me. Worse still I also saw my friends become *humanized*—I will explain more about becoming humanized in the next chapter—and take on some or all of these behaviours and opinions.

I fought this humanization for a few short years and felt a sort of pride in doing so. In some small way I thought that, if I was to carry on with what I knew and not become humanized, I would perhaps be able to change other people's opinions or beliefs. I strongly held on to this for as long as possible, even though it did affect my socializing with the other kids. Don't get me wrong, I was not an outcast; I had a small circle of friends and knew a lot of other school friends as acquaintances, but I was not always invited to all the other children's birthday parties, and I was not always allowed to participate in the sports or games that others were playing.

Some children were polite but definitely kept me at arms length; I could tell that they were unsure about me, but I was fine with that, for I still believed that one day I would be able to help them with my story—I just didn't know it would be over thirty-five years later! At eight years old I seriously began to have doubts that what I knew would make any difference at all, and at around ten years of age I gave in to the human peer pressure and became humanized, more accepted and able to join in—I felt that I belonged, although deep down I knew it was the wrong sort of belonging. From here to teenage years I changed quite considerably but not necessarily for the better.

My Teenage Years

It was now the '80s, and after leaving primary school and entering secondary school at the age of eleven, things changed quite dramatically. I could already see the difference in the behaviour of my schoolmates; they were turning away from childhood interests and pursuing more adult interests, including smoking, drinking and the inquisitive nature that goes with it.

I had left my memory behind the best that I could, and I was now being readily accepted by my peers and being involved with more clubs and sports teams. I finally felt I had a sense of belonging, and I felt quite liberated. I tried pushing my memory to the back of my mind in order to continue on with my journey of being a 'normal' teenager.

Roll on two or three years, and I am now about thirteen or fourteen years old. I had done some pretty neat stuff; I was on the school soccer team, the school basketball team, the school rugby team, and the school athletic team, throwing the shot putt. I also played soccer on representative teams in my age group for local towns. I had also worked in market stalls at our local market and with my dad doing small landscaping jobs. Unfortunately, I had done some pretty silly stuff as well; I had tried smoking, drank alcohol, had a few fights, played truant from school, was becoming troublesome in the classes at school that I did attend and had started some rebellious behaviour. Some of this I put down to being an exploratory teenager, and some of it I put down to trying to stay free of my memory and the things I knew that I should not be doing—but hey, these things were making me popular, and that is what's important, right?

Moving forward two more years and I was still doing most of the pretty neat stuff mentioned before and making a bit of a name for myself playing soccer, but the pretty silly stuff had also risen more, and now I was well behind on school-work, out most nights with my mates drinking alcohol and smoking, and generally believing that moving in this direction would enhance my popularity and banish away those early years as a child where my memory had made me feel slightly as an outsider. Oh and now I was a punk—punk rock never dies eh!

Fast forward just a few months, and things had now turned pear shaped. I dislocated my shoulder playing around at school, and any dreams or desires of pursuing a soccer career were gone. My schoolwork was pretty much non-existent, and I was due to leave school within the next three months. What now? Well, I can answer that question for you quite easily. What it meant was that I would now have to leave school, find a job and work hard, but earning a wage would also mean I could party harder. It meant that, as I was no longer involved with soccer, I didn't have the responsibility of training and staying in shape. Last but not least, it meant lots of late nights and significant hangovers in the mornings. At the back of my mind I still knew that I was using a lot of this behaviour to hide away my memory, but I was a popular guy, so why would I want to jeopardize all that again?

My Early Adult Life

By the time I was eighteen years old, I was working as a labourer on construction sites and living the typical young adult lifestyle, spending my time socializing with my mates at local clubs, pubs and nightclubs. Weekdays were for working and seemed to take an eternity to go by. Weeknights were for socializing with a limit on the drinking due to work restraints. Weekends were for partying and were just a blur. From the outside everything looked rosy, but from the inside, even though I was enjoying living this carefree life, I still had my memory knocking on the door every now and again, telling me that some of the things I was doing were not right and that perhaps one day—perhaps *someday*—I might have the courage to release what I knew about my memory to the world.

A couple of months before my nineteenth birthday, things changed dramatically—I fell in love! I had different girlfriends throughout my teenage and early adult years, but this young lady was different. Almost from the off I was smitten. We met at a local nightclub, and—I will always remember this—she asked me my astrological sign. Luckily I was a Pisces and not an Aries, otherwise she said she would not have dated me as our star signs would not have worked together. I could see and hear from the way she spoke that she was herself quite a spiritual person. Things were looking up. I still was not brave enough to tell her all about my memory, but I could talk to her in such a way that included things from my memory, and we could have some really interesting and insightful conversations without me having to confess what it is that I had been carrying around with me my whole life.

My new girlfriend was an au pair, looking after two young children. She worked and lived with a family about twelve miles away from my home, so we frequently went out together, saw each other and just hung out as a couple. After three months her contract with this family had come to an end and we moved in together. I was nineteen, and she was twenty.

After three years of living together we married had our two lovely children, a son and a daughter, and suffered the loss of another baby through a miscarriage—more about this in the sub-chapter on Coping With Loss in chapter eight called Why Did I Write This Book Now. We worked, holidayed in Denmark—this is where my wife comes from originally and where her family still lives—and generally went about our business with the focus of buying our home, raising our family and having as much quality time together as we could.

During this time I was no longer employed by the same company that I had worked with for seven years, due to the recession that swept through the UK in the early '90s, and I now worked for myself, running my own business as a landscape gardener; my wife worked in a payroll office. We were both happy with our jobs, but we also both had ambition to be as successful as we could be in our careers. My wife was being frequently promoted within her office and soon got to the position of managing teams. For me it was slightly different. All the time I had worked in the construction industry, from being a labourer to running my own business, I had wanted to have my own larger landscape company. Now, all of a sudden and completely out of the blue, I wanted a career change. I wanted to help people who had issues going on in their lives and needed assistance to deal with these issues so that they could move on positively with their lives. It felt as though this was the first time in many years that I had decided to let my memory come back in and influence me slightly.

I thought about this possible life-changing decision long and hard, after all I had a successful business operating and lots of good clients. I made the choice that I wanted to work with teenagers with problems; it seemed appropriate considering how my own teenage years had turned out. I decided to volunteer at a youth project in our local town a couple of mornings a week to see whether I would like to work in this profession or not. This way I could still run by business and earn a living landscaping until I had made up my mind. I started volunteering and soon realized that I really enjoyed helping people and was able to put some of my memory teachings into practice within this position without anyone noticing. I was also able to draw on some of the experiences from my own teenage years. A short time later, a big decision was made, and I started working at another youth project that paid a wage, whilst still volunteering at the first youth project. I also enrolled myself at our local college and started on the road to getting my Humanistic Counselling Diploma.

The Rest Of My Adult Years Until We Immigrated To Canada

While studying to become a counsellor, I changed jobs and took on a full time position as a Youth Worker at a new youth agency that started up in our town. The hours worked very well for me, and I was able to fit in my college days and continue towards my chosen goal. The job involved working with youth who had issues regarding homelessness, drugs or alcohol, sexual health, unemployment—a real mix of issues that young people may go through in their lives. I really enjoyed this job and once again found that using the knowledge from my memory was helpful in assisting these young people. I enjoy a laugh and a joke and found that using humour, in the right context and at the right time, could also be beneficial to them. Some of the young people I saw really did not have a lot to laugh about, so working in this manner helped them to break the rigidity of coming to an office and gave them a breath of fresh air.

It was during this time that I managed to get a placement at a local Alcohol Counselling facility, so I stopped working as a volunteer at the first youth agency and swapped my hours to the alcohol facility instead. What with work, volunteering, college and raising a family things were getting quite busy!

After three years of studying and doing my counselling placement I passed my Humanistic Counselling Diploma and was a very happy bunny indeed. I had relinquished the ghosts of school and, through my own hard work and determination, had achieved a higher level of education; something I would never have dreamt possible when I left school. I obtained a job in a Domestic Abuse Project working with both women and men who had been the victims of domestic abuse, and who either had drug or alcohol issues or were living in a drug or alcohol environment. I stopped working at the second youth agency and the alcohol facility. By now my wife had been promoted to Payroll Manager, and this seemed to be our life mapped out in front of us. But then we visited Canada!

My sister had immigrated to Canada in the late '80s, and I had visited once on my own in 1997 to be a godfather at my niece's christening. In 2001 we all came over on a family holiday, to visit my sister and her family, and fell in love with Canada. While riding on a chairlift down Grouse Mountain, we all decided that we would like to move here. After our holiday was over we returned back home to the UK and we sent in our application to immigrate to Canada, all the while having to get on with our everyday lives. After two years we finally got our visas and were elated; we could now move to Canada. We left the UK for Vancouver Island around four months later and have not looked back since.

My Life In Canada So Far

When we arrived in Canada, we stayed at my sister's house in Vancouver for a week before heading off to Vancouver Island to look for our new home. We rented a lake house for a couple of months, just so we could have a bit of a holiday and enjoy getting into the Canadian way of life, before buying our first home here in Canada. We settled our children into their new school, and I went on a job hunting mission. For the first eight months here I worked as a support worker at a local FASD (Fetal Alcohol Spectrum Disorder) project but found that the work I really wanted to do, to be a counsellor, was difficult to get into because my counselling diploma was not recognized here; I would have to redo my studies. I thought about it quite a lot but, in the end, decided against doing that. Instead I started a landscaping business, and my wife retrained as a Realtor.

We carried on with our new lives here in Canada. Our children made friends and became involved with sports and dance clubs, and my wife and I also made friends and began enjoying Canadian living. I still had my memory with me, but that's where it stayed—with me. We have had some great adventures here and enjoyed vacations up and down Vancouver Island, across British Columbia, in various parts of the United States. We've returned back to Europe to visit family and friends in both the UK and Denmark. We love living here and have no regrets about moving halfway around the world for our new home.

This brings me and my *memory* up to the present day!

CHAPTER 2

So What Is My Memory?

WHAT I AM ABOUT TO WRITE ABOUT HAS LITERALLY BEEN WITH ME forever. It has been a part of me since day one, yet it has taken me all this time to begin to share it with anyone. I am now forty-four years old and have only recently told my wife, my children and a couple of friends. As I sit down to write this, the sum total of people who know what I am about to divulge is eight—plus me of course.

Telling anyone something that is out of the ordinary is very hard. This is true for any subject, not just what I am writing about. Writing this book would have been very daunting not too long ago—perhaps almost impossible—but now I feel ready and willing to do so.

A major reason for not telling anyone about my memory is that I was always unsure of how people would react. As humans we never know fully how people may react to certain news, and this has definitely played on my mind for years. I think that more and more people now are accepting of spirituality and New Age beliefs, and I suppose my memory would fall under these headings—although once you know what my memory is you will see it is not actually New Age. It has been with all of us since the beginning of time.

I can remember many things from the past and quite a way back into my childhood. I have early memories of being four or five years old that have stayed in my brain for many years, and I have generally always had a good long-term memory. Sometimes this can be useful and beneficial, but sometimes it can seem a little pointless—after all, why would I want to remember a jingle from a television advert from the 1970s? Perhaps there will be a reason for remembering this jingle one day. My short-term memory on the other hand has not always been so good… now where was I? Oh yes, my long-term memory. So what is my memory?

Okay, here goes…

I can remember before I was born. *There*, I've said it!

When I say *I can remember before I was born*, I mean just that. I can remember BEFORE I was born. I am not talking about the moment just before birth when I left my mother's womb. Nor am I talking about living in a past life. I am talking about before I was born, *in between lives* if you like. It is the most amazing place; where you go *after* you leave your previous life and *before* you enter your next life. It is where we all were before we found ourselves here on Earth. I call it a Prior Life experience.

Prior Life Experience

A Prior Life experience is just that, the experience prior to life. As a child I had very vivid memories and recollections of my time before becoming a human being on Earth. These memories were very powerful and, in some sense, gave me a feeling of safety because of what they represented. In another sense they left me a little confused and feeling slightly alone, for I did not feel comfortable sharing them with anyone.

Between me thinking that I had to keep my memory silent and my trying to shut this experience out, while moving forwards with my life, I can not remember everything as clearly as I could as a child, but I do have recollections of my Prior Life that have been indelibly etched into my brain. Regardless of how much I tried to close the door on them over the years, these specific strong memories of my Prior Life experience have remained clear in my mind. Our Prior Life is a wonderful and pleasant experience and should not be feared in any way; on the contrary, it should be revered in all its glory, for it is a comforting time for us, shared together in a great place. It is a very safe experience and one that we have all been through and will go through again. For a long time I felt cursed that I could remember my Prior Life experience, but now I feel lucky, for I now feel that it is a gift that has been bestowed upon me, one which I am now willing to share with the world.

When I used to sit and think about the memories from my Prior Life experience, I did wonder what people would think of them if I was ever to open up and share them. I wondered if people would understand them and their intrinsic message. But for years wonder was all I did, for I kept those memories locked away. Now I am confident that it is the right time and that there will be more understanding surrounding them.

I remember watching a comedy movie with my family a few years ago. I cannot remember the name of the movie, but the storyline involved a guy who was born without his memory being erased by his angel. This left him with memories of his previous life; that caused a few problems and issues in his new life. The angel who was supposed to erase his memory was sent to earth to do so years later, after the guy had grown into a man. Although this movie is not portraying the exact same history of my memory, I did have my own private laughs at what was being shown in this movie, for I remembered my own Prior Life experience, and thought to myself, *if only they knew*. I did not have the courage to tell my family at that stage, so I continued to keep my memory safe within me. I would love to see this movie again and share my private laughs with the people who I have told about my memory—I just need to remember what the movie was called!

My wife has asked me about the timescale of my Prior Life experience, and I can only answer from what I know. I do not remember my previous life or any past lives previous to that, and as I mentioned earlier, I cannot remember my birth. The time that I remember is exactly between lives. It is the time after my previous life and before this present one. Nor do I remember any other *previous* Prior Life experiences, only the one before coming to my current human existence. Regarding timescales, I do not know if I was there for the human timescale equivalent of one day, one year, one decade, one century or any other unit of time. From my own memories, having a Prior Life experience does not have a time factor or time limit attached to it. It is not like we are quick-change artists or fashion models on a runway, who have a fixed amount of time to get changed from one outfit to the other before the next set or catwalk. With Prior Life we have all the time we need and return to life when we are ready. It is not like the delicatessen counter in the local supermarket where you take a ticket and sit and wait in a line. Everything will happen *and has happened* at the correct time space scenario for each of us. Time does not have any meaning in Prior Life; what has meaning is what we are learning from life; what we learnt from previous lives and what we want to learn in this one—I will talk about this with more detail in this chapter under the sub-header called The Room.

Even though I have kept my Prior Life experience and memories hidden for my entire life, I am now happy that I have them. They no longer seem like a bane for me, a thorn in my side. I now see them as being a special gift. A gift that I have been able to learn from—and a gift that I am very willing to now share.

Having a Prior Life experience is something that we have all had, and just because you can not remember it, does not mean you did not have it. If I were to ask you to tell me about every single day of your life starting from day one you would be pretty stumped, yet you know that these days happened, otherwise you would not be here now reading this book.

I can recall my Prior Life as being an exciting time, and where we are during Prior Life is absolutely awesome in the place I call The Room. I will tell you all that I can remember and recall from my time in The Room before my birth.

The Room

As a young child growing up, I had tremendous memories of The Room. The Room is an amazing place with such a powerfully safe feeling that flows within it. It is warm, comfortable, friendly, loving, happy, non-judgmental and exciting— imagine every positive emotion you've ever experienced and multiply that many times over. There are no judgments, jealousies or competition between us as spirit energies in The Room, and the feeling of love there is so immense that writing about it here in this book does not do it justice. The Room is a wonderful place to be, and the thought of returning to it one day holds no fear for me. I know where we came from before this human life, and I know where we will return to after it.

The Room is a special place, and it provides complete peace, stillness and tranquility. When I hear people talk about Heaven, it sounds very much to me like my memory of The Room. It is an outstanding place, and as much as I can try here in this book, words can not amply describe it. The Room could be described as an area, but I have never felt that being called an area is suitable for such a special and amazing place, so I have always referred to it as The Room, even when thinking about it myself before telling anyone of my memory.

My wife has spoken to me a lot about The Room, since I told her of my memory. She said to me that she would like to try and have a taste of what it is like in The Room. She has asked me to try and help her better understand my experience of existing in The Room. For that reason I devised an exercise to help her have an *in-The-Room* experience. I would like to share this exercise with you so that you can try it for yourself and have your own *in-The-Room* experience and share this experience with others.

Please find a quiet place, away from noise or other distractions. You can either sit or lie down, whatever is better for you. I would like you to close your eyes and completely relax. Take a couple of deep breaths, and then slow down your breathing. Allow yourself to drift into a meditative state if you desire—any relaxed, calm state of mind is sufficient. Once you are nice and comfortable, please think back about one of the happiest moments you have had in your life. It can be of anything at all just so long as it is a *happy* moment from your past. When you are thinking about this happy moment and re-living those good memories and feelings, multiply that feeling by ten. Then think about that happy moment in time some more and with greater detail and multiply that feeling by ten again. While you are in your chosen moment keep thinking about that very happy memory in depth and multiply the feeling by another ten. Keep this happy memory flowing and multiply the feeling by ten again, then ten again, then ten again.

This exercise could go on and on forever and ever, even multiplying the feeling by ten each time, because the feeling of compassion, non-judgment, happiness, excitement and belonging are so strong in The Room that trying to match it completely is a huge task. This exercise just gives a very small taste of what it is like in The Room, but at least a very small taste still gives some of the positive experience of being there and some understanding of what The Room entails.

I have specific memories from The Room that I would like to share with you here. I can remember being in a smaller space with another energy spirit. This energy spirit was more like a teacher, and I remember being very comfortable in their presence. In front of both me and the teacher is a large Journal that has the details of my previous lives and my choices for my life ahead. So you see, the term *life choices* are more real than you think! I cannot remember what is in the Journal for my previous lives or this life, but I know I am happy with what I have done before in previous lives and what I will aim for in this one. I am not sure that I remembered details from the Journal when I was a child, but if I did this would have been one of the more specific memories that I put away. If I still have it somewhere, perhaps one day it will resurface and show itself to me again, and if not, then I do not need it.

Outside this smaller space is a larger space—what I refer to as The Room. Here in The Room it is full of spirit energies—like myself—who are all on different levels and life journeys. I say *full of spirit energies,* but it is difficult to quantify the number of spirit energies there; in my memory the whole area is a thriving, contiguous mass of spirit energy. I remember *communication* but not as we know it on Earth, it was more akin to communicating by intuition. It is interesting that, here on Earth, we have many different languages and sublanguages requiring translation in order to be understood; in The Room there is one common way of communicating and this is done easily, readily and intuitively by all.

I have been asked by my wife to describe what the spirit energies look like and this is a difficult question to answer—they weren't physical entities more like energy/colour beings—but I will answer it as best I can. When I think of the spirit energy around me in The Room I see them as a very light colour—like a mix between white, cream and yellow. It is not an actual colour that we know and can name—like blue for example—but a bright whitey, creamy, light yellowy colour. I see the spirit energies' shape as not an exact shape, but somewhere near the shape of an upside down egg carton. If you turn an egg carton upside down and look at the twelve egg pockets that are now facing the ceiling, one of these egg pockets is similar to the shape that I see in my mind's eye—so looking at all twelve egg pockets would be similar to looking at twelve energy spirits. As I said it is not an exact shape—they are indistinct—it's just the closest way I can describe their shape without having anything else to compare it to. Even though it may not be an exact replica of how I see spirit energy, I hope that my descriptions will at least give you some idea of how they are and how we were *and will be again*. My wife said she is happy to be an egg pocket!

I have a tremendous memory of what it is like to witness a spirit energy leaving The Room to be born to this world. It is a very exciting and inspiring time and one that is enjoyed and shared between the spirit energy being born and every other spirit energy around. The best way I have found to describe this is that it is like the scene from the movie *Toy Story*, where the Martian toys are all standing inside an amusement arcade machine and are waiting to be chosen by 'the claw'. When someone puts their money in and plays the machine and the claw lowers down and grabs a Martian toy, all the other toys are so happy for the Martian toy chosen and wish it well. This is true of The Room and all the spirit energies there.

When it is time for a spirit energy to leave The Room and be born to this human existence all the other spirit energies wish the onward spirit all the best, and there is no envy, hate or disdain—only love, happiness and vicarious pleasure for the departing spirit. I can remember being around for a few times when spirit energy departed from The Room to be born to this world, and they were truly heart-warming times. I can distinctly remember when it was my turn to leave and I received the best wishes from the other spirit energies—the feeling of excitement that I had as I began my journey to this earth was astounding. I knew that I was heading into my human existence and that this experience in and of itself would be amazing. This excitement stayed with me through my early childhood as I remembered The Room, but as I began to realize that I was the only one with this memory, it was slowly humanized out. When I think of how excitable small children can be, it makes me think that their natural exuberance and energy is a carryover from their time in The Room.

My wife has asked me why we are born and what do we come to Earth as human beings to learn? From my memories I cannot answer these questions fully, but I do know that in the Journal that I am looking at with the teacher, there are things both from my previous life experience plus my next life—which of course is this life I am on now. To me this suggests that we have been here before and will be here again. I cannot remember exact details of what is in the Journal—and I have tried through concentration and meditation—but I now believe that it is probably best that I do not know so that I can live my life, allowing things to flow naturally, instead of trying to force things into my life because the Journal said it would happen. Anything that is supposed to happen will happen, and I am now more comfortable just being. Perhaps, when I return to The Room and look at that Journal with the teacher again, it will show that I wrote *this book* that you are now reading.

As to why we come to Earth—our purpose—again I can answer this a little bit more from my memories. When I think back to The Room, I understand that we, spirit energies, are on a continuing journey. We come to Earth as human beings to learn from that journey. As I said earlier, I do remember communicating with spirit energies that were on *different* levels; what level I was on I do not know, but I know that there were higher levels for me to achieve which suggested that my own journey was far from over. One thing I would like to point out is that, though spirit energies exist on different levels, there is no judgment based on levels. There is only love and support, and I can remember having these feelings from the higher level spirit energies in The Room.

My time in The Room has come to the forefront of my mind at various times during my life. Sometimes it has been there every day, a few times a day, for a while. Other times it has not been there for a few days, but I do know that all I have to do is think about it and the memories of The Room comes flooding back. When I was younger, before becoming humanized—I will explain more about becoming humanized in the next sub header—I found this to be of some relief to me. It was like having my own inner security blanket. As

I grew older, through teenage and my early adult years, it became more of a burden. Now that I have accepted it more and shared it with others, I am beginning to feel more secure with my Prior Life experience, and The Room is beginning to feel very much like my safe place once more.

From now on I will treasure my memories from The Room and feel honoured that I still have them. They are amazing memories—and I have always *known* that—but now I am beginning to appreciate that as well. I am appreciating the memories as being a gift, bearing important insights. I am accepting that it is okay to have these Prior Life memories, and it is even better to share them for the benefit of others so that everyone can better understand how it was—and will be again—in The Room.

Becoming Humanized

When we are born, we are still spiritual beings, but as we grow, we take on the appearances, traits and opinions of other humans around us like family, friends and those who influence us through culture and media. This is commonly known as socialization but I think it is more than that—I call it becoming *humanized*. As a young child, I still had a certain amount of free will. Yes, my parents and friends may have had some influence and input into my life, but I still remember clearly which of these influences I wanted to take on and which ones I could not understand from an in-The-Room perspective. For instance I could not understand why people would argue or fight and why some people thought bullying was necessary. I enjoyed watching sports for the fun of the game, yet I can remember feeling that it was strange when people would boo and jeer opposing teams. Even if people were ecstatic that their team had won, why was it necessary to verbally abuse the opponents? Why would people call each other names? Why would they be nasty to animals? Why would countries go to war against each other? Why would people have enemies? Why this? Why that? Why? Why? Why?

I can clearly remember having these thoughts and feelings and the bewilderment that went with them, after all I was looking from an in-The-Room point of view, and these things simply did not happen there. Unfortunately, I can also remember becoming more and more humanized—slowly moving away from the knowledge that I had inside me from The Room and moving into the thoughts and patterns of the majority. It was as though I felt I had to become humanized just to get along in this life. I had tried living my life according to in-The-Room precepts, but it had no affect on anyone around me and I had not found anyone else who was sharing the Prior Life experience that I had. So I started to believe that arguing was fine. If an argument ended up in a fight, well—as the stereotype suggests—*boys will be boys*. And so I would hurl abuse at any opposing sports teams regardless of whether my team won, lost, played well or played badly— so long as I could either gloat in victory or verbalize my anger towards the opposition in defeat then all was right in the world.

I know that, in my life, I have been told by other people that it is okay to do something that is not right—out of line with my in-The-Room memories—because all these bad things may happen to me one day. Every bad thing seemed to have a a built-in justification. *Survival of The Fittest* was a saying that was batted around a lot at the time. One thing I have come to recognize, looking back over my life, is the fear that we human beings have. I did not notice it at the time, but now I see how fear-based human society has become and how most people live according to their fears. Becoming humanized opened up the door to a lot of fears—fears imposed upon us from different aspects of society. Often times there can be too great a focus on the fear of something bad happening—something that may never come to pass— and far too little focus on enjoying life and getting on with the journey. Nowadays I try and keep my thoughts away from any of these negative societal thoughts and steer clear of fear-based discussion. I would rather be actively involved with something I like doing than passively sitting around and discussing my fears; that is how fear increases. Think positive, talk positive and spread positive—I know that is how I want to live.

We are one of those families that do not watch the news; we know that any news that we are supposed to know will come to us. We are not burying our head in the sand or denying that these news stories are happening, but we instead choose not to feed into any negatives that may be in the news. We will pass on positive news stories to others as we believe in sharing the positive. Remember, in The Room there is only positive, so negatives and fears do not exist within us there. As a family we are happy not to have them exist with us here. Please do not get me wrong, becoming humanized is not all negative, there are positive aspects which allow us to live as humans here on Earth. When I talk about negative aspects of humanization, I am referring to negative, fear-based behaviours and emotions; they are the things that I want to leave behind. They are the things I do not want to own.

For me becoming humanized became a way of fitting in and moving along with my human life. It was about being accepted and trying to accept that this was the human way and that my old in-The-Room way was not appropriate for life on Earth. Slowly my memories of being in The Room and what I call Prior Life experiences were closed down and packed away—boxed up as *not useful* for my time on this Earth. But throughout it all, there have been the stronger memories and feelings I experienced—those that could be neither squashed nor extinguished—and they are what I am writing about in this book. Forty-four years after my birth, I am so pleased that they stayed with me; I hope to be able to recollect some of the other memories.

Now I am not afraid of others' opinions, I am not scared of what others think, and I do not fear what people might say about me. Now I can understand fully what my knowledge of The Room may mean to humankind. I am so thankful that I have the courage to share it with the rest of the world and hope that it will benefit a lot of people and help make the world a better place. Becoming humanized was a big occasion in my life—as it is for all of us—but having the knowledge from The Room to *support* that humanization is essential if we are to maintain perspective. It allows us to face the process of humanization with our eyes open, choosing which parts of becoming humanized we wish to take on and which parts we do not.

Human Feelings

In The Room only positive feelings exist. Love, warmth, happiness, and acceptance are ubiquitous there; they are a never-ending constant and universal to all. Of course these are also human feelings, but the human spectrum of feeling also includes negative feelings such as hate, fear, judgments, exclusion, blame and guilt, which only manifest themselves here on Earth. If we can learn to live with the positive in-The-Room feelings and keep out the negative manifested human feelings, we will all benefit. When we promote positivity towards other people, we feel positive ourselves; if we send out negative messages, we attract negativity.

We can all learn to embrace our in-The-Room feelings and get back to our warm, secure, confident, natural pre-humanized state. The in-The-Room experience is too amazing and powerful for words, and if we strive to embody it we will enhance our lives dramatically, secure in the knowledge of where it was we came from and where it is we will one day return. We have all had inklings of a Prior Life experience and we can all manifest these feelings again. We do not have to wait until we return to The Room to experience the joy of these feelings again.

Peer Pressure And Role Models

While we are here on earth, living a human existence, the lives of our fellow human beings exert significant influence on us. This influence can come in one of two ways: the influence of peer pressure or the influence of role models. Peer pressure is about being compelled to do something that feels counter-intuitive— it is generally harmful or negative in some way e. g. smoking or drugs. I know that peer pressure from friends is why I first started smoking. Once we succumb to peer pressure we then inevitably propagate it by imposing it on other peers—getting other friends to smoke for instance.

I have seen how peer pressure can negatively affect an individual, involving them in stuff they would otherwise avoid. Conversely I have also seen how it—negatively—enables a group by swelling its ranks and thus further justifying its own destructive behaviour. I admit that I have done this in my smoking days—not wanting to give up my own habit and pressuring friends who wanted to quit so that they would reconsider. Being surrounded by smokers made my smoking easier. I can honestly say I am not proud of this.

Peer pressure can also involve other people imposing their opinion of another person onto you. Whatever another person's thought are about a third party, you cannot let that affect how you feel about that particular person. When you allow this to happen, what you are doing is forming a second-hand opinion and not giving the individual in question a chance to make his or her own impression. Do not play Chinese whispers with other people's lives. Trust yourself to form your own opinions. Remember that your own thoughts, feelings and opinions are most important to you.

A role model is someone who inspires us to take on a particular role for a greater good. This may be through competing in a sport, through singing or music, through working in a particular profession or just about any other positive action you can think of. Role models are looked up to by others and are generally involved in positive aspects of life. I have witnessed changes in people who have become inspired by role models and have taken on their own true beliefs that they can do what their role model has shown them. As a teenager my role models were soccer players. It didn't matter whether they were famous, local players for our home town teams or friends I knew my own age. I know that my teenage years would have been a lot more troubled if I did not have soccer to give me some focus in life. Watching and learning from soccer role models helped me to take my soccer to as high a level as I did before my injury.

In The Room there is no peer pressure; we all support each other to enhance all our particular journeys. No one is pressured to do anything that runs counter to their best interests. It is interesting that in The Room there aren't role models *per se* because everyone is equal and does whatever they can to benefit each other—but there are *teachers* who help us with our journeys. If there is a positive role for peer pressure to play in the earthly lives of humans, it is to encourage potential role models to step forward and inspire others to follow their own best instincts—making them less susceptible to negative peer pressure.

Chapter 3

Valuable Lessons From The Room

When I think back to my time in The Room, I remember the valuable insights that are so helpful for us in our lives on this Earth. These are precious tools that we can use in our everyday lives. We can share them with others and assist others in using these lessons— making our time here on Earth better, more fun, more positive and more like the place we left and will return to one day, The Room.

Love

When I think back to my Prior Life experience and my longest memories, the place where love shines through the most clearly is in The Room. Love is the foundation of The Room and the very essence of our spiritual energy. In The Room there is only love. Nothing stands in contrast or opposition to love in The Room—whereas here on Earth these contrasts are all around us. The Beatles sang "All You Need Is Love," and that is so true; I know that here on Earth we have also basic needs such as food, water and shelter, but when we return to The Room love is all we will need. If we can put a little more emphasis on love and make it as important as the basic human needs, we can nourish both our human bodies and our spiritual energy—our soul.

When we think about love and who we should love, a few common themes come up. There is our family to love: our wives, husbands, sons, daughters, parents, siblings and our extended family. There are our friends to love, those near and dear to us. There are our pets to love. There are even co-workers and acquaintances to love. All of these beings form themes and patterns in our lives which most of us naturally understand. But there are the other not-so-common themes when it comes to love. We can love the homeless and those less fortunate than ourselves. We can love those in countries devastated by war, famine or natural disasters. We can love strangers. Most notably, we can love the people we may have hated; we can love our enemies. I am using the word enemy but you should know that it is purely an earthly concept; in The Room enemies do not exist.

We can spend so much precious time hating others that we lose focus on our own lives. We can get so engrossed with the misery of those we hate that our life passes us by and we miss so much of the beauty that is going on around us every day. We can get so caught up in revenge that we fail to notice how it may affect our physical and mental health. Even blessed with my knowledge from The Room, I know I have fallen prey to this sort of thing from time to time. Thankfully I have learned to pass these feelings by for they do no one any good. The fleeting gratification they provide is entirely superficial.

It is far easier—and more rewarding—to spread the positivity of love; this is our true element from spirit energy. When we send out love and provide harmony to others, we give ourselves the opportunity to receive love and benefit from harmony in our own lives. We are able to focus on how we want to live; we can see and appreciate the wonders of this world and feel better physically and mentally—rather than struggling to live with the twisted, intense behaviour of hate. There is another song called "Love Is All Around Us" by The Troggs—and indeed it is. Tap into this love; accept this love; give out this love, and promote this love. The more we love, the more love there is in the world—and the more love there is in the world, the better.

Important Qualities

We all have important qualities within us that we need to accept and be proud of. It is not about being arrogant or self-centred. It does not mean you are big headed. Instead it is about being confident and proud. It means you have a quality to give, and we all do! So much is put onto us from society—how we should be and not be—that sometimes people do not want to stand out in a certain way, or talk about how good they are at something in case they go against society's grain and look bad. I have been in this box throughout my life with my memory, but I now refuse to be in this box anymore. I am willing to put here in writing that what I have to offer is important. One of my most important qualities—and it has served me throughout my life—is my ability to listen to others and offer support. This is probably what led me to a career as a counsellor. I can remember sitting down on park benches and having total strangers come and sit down next to me; they would start talking to me about the weather or how their day was going and continue talking until they had almost told me their whole life story within five minutes. I have always felt pretty good with myself, knowing that the energy I give out is taken in this way, and that people feel comfortable sharing things with me, even if they have never met me before.

Furthermore, it makes me proud to write it—and happy to read it. I am not boasting or being big headed; I am just sharing and being honest. Be proud of your important qualities; do not be afraid to share them. Every important quality shared is a positive shared; and every positive shared means more positive energy surrounding and connecting us all. As human beings we are quite comfortable to talk to others about what we cannot do. Instead we should now be confident and proud of what we can do and voice it to others with confidence.

And as we let our own light shine, we unconsciously give other people permission to do the same. —Nelson Mandela

Deny Ego

As humans we have certain elements that make up our physical and psychological beings. One of those elements is called the ego. The ego is often known as the false self. We all want to do the best we can and achieve the most we can achieve, and there is nothing wrong with that. Where it becomes an issue is when self-importance overtakes the desire for success. By this I mean that success and recognition is still sought after by the person, but now to serve different needs. It is the need to look a particular way in one's own mind and in the eyes of others. It is about having a false ideal of who you are, and putting yourself fundamentally above other people. When this occurs—and fairness and equality crumble—the true self is smothered by the ego and false self.

Be successful and achieve all that you want to achieve, and be the best you can, and do all that you want to do. Please, live your life to the fullest. Just be aware of who you truly are, of where you came from, and where you are returning to. Be gracious with success, not egotistical. The ego exists within all of us, and it is how we deal with our ego that is important. When we were all having our Prior Life experiences in The Room, there was no such a thing as an ego. Let us all keep our egos under control while we are living our human lives.

> *Egoism and competition are, alas, stronger forces than public spirit and sense of duty.* —Albert Einstein

Look Inside And See Yourself

We can look at ourselves in the mirror every day and change how we want to be. We can change our hairstyle, our hair colour, our clothes and our shoes. We can decide whether to shave or not, and we can decide to put makeup on or not. That is our external self that we present to the word—and ourselves—every day. Then there is our internal self. Our internal self can be seen by both us and other people. We know whether the person we are portraying to the outside world is authentic or not. The outside world can see the person being projected and will inevitably draw their own conclusions and opinions about them.

I know that there have times in my life when I have been proud of myself: my behaviour, appearance or what I may have done for others. There have been times when I have been embarrassed about my behaviour, my appearance and how I may have treated other people.

I have realized that I do not have to bow to other people's perceptions or judgments. I have realized that I do not have to give in to my ego. I have realized that I am in control of my life, and I can be who I want to be. You can do this too. Look inside yourself and find your authentic self—allow your authentic self to be free. Live the life that you want, and be who you want to be.

It took me a long time to look inside and see myself clearly, but I know that once I did it was easy to keep track of who I was. I can look inside of myself whenever I desire, and I encourage you to do the same. For me, looking inside of myself takes me back to that time in The Room when I was genuine being who I was. Now I can be who I am.

The snow goose need not bathe to make itself white. Neither need you do anything but be yourself. —Lao Tzu

Look Inside And See The Other Person

When I worked as a counsellor, I used to see people who had issues with drugs, alcohol, homelessness and abuse of all kinds. The person that sat before me was not the person I counselled. I looked past the shell of the human being that was sitting before me and looked at the person who really was inside. Many people may have difficulties with a variety of issues in their lives. While going through these issues, people may looked bedraggled, unwashed, frustrated or fearful, but this is not who they are. Underneath is the real them, the person who has had happiness and success in their life but are now struggling. We shouldn't judge someone based on the way they look or present themselves—looks and presentation change. Seeing someone change through counselling is an uplifting experience.

I have looked inside the person many times during my counselling career. I remember a female client who came for counselling because her ex-husband was an alcoholic and kept causing trouble for her and her children, even though he was no longer living in the family home. Her confidence was very low; she was frustrated at his behaviour and her inability to deal with it. When she first walked into the counselling room, I saw her appearance and can only refer to it as *mousey*. She looked and dressed as though she were a lot older than she actually was and walked hurriedly and slightly bent over. Throughout the twelve counselling sessions she was able to work through different issues that she had with her ex-husband, looked at safety issues for her and her children in terms of contacting the police, and reviewed what she wanted from life from this point onwards. By the end of the twelfth session she looked like a completely different woman. She walked upright, at a more normal speed. The way she dressed was very fashionable, and her hair was much more fitting for her. In fact I would go as far to say she looked quite glamorous at her final session. Had I made judgements or assumptions about the woman she was based on her initial appearance I would have been woefully off-base, but coming both from my Prior Life experience and my role as a counsellor, I chose not to. Instead I looked inside to see the real person.

Empathy

This is a very important quality for all humankind. Empathy is one of the softest and kindest words I know, but is also one of the strongest words. Empathy is a word that means the ability to share or understand the emotions and feelings of another person. I find that very powerful. In counselling, empathy is crucial to the process. It is important to allow the other person to know that they are being listened to and understood, for they are able to move on with their lives with this type of support. When we are in The Room, we are at our most empathic. We are all thinking about one another, caring about one another, and looking after one another. We are connected, we are all one. Empathy here on Earth allows that in-The-Room compassion I am talking about, and once we are all able to be more empathic to one another we will be able to continue with a more caring and positive world. Being empathic is natural for us as spirit energy in The Room, so let us naturally continue being empathic here on Earth as human beings.

Being A Rescuer

I have tended to be a rescuer for most of my life—as far back as I can remember. I am talking here about both physical and emotional rescue. Bullying is one of the things that I have always had a personal gripe with. I remember once, when I was around eight or nine years old—and just starting to deny my Prior Life memories—deciding that I should perhaps try to be a bully. I myself had been bullied, and bullying was going on around me. I tried bullying one boy, but found it was so unnatural that I instantly became focused against bullying. If I saw bullying going on at school, I would be willing to intervene and take on the role of the rescuer.

As an emotional rescuer, I have always been a listener and felt compassion towards people, so my career as a counsellor was perfect for me. In both my personal and professional life,

I have been a shoulder to cry on, an advocate, a confidante and even put myself out there as an emotional punching bag. I have been a listening ear and a voice to speak out for. One thing I have often done is help people out in group conversations if they are having awkward moments, for example if they cannot think of what to say or are getting flummoxed—or if there are long silences or one way conversations are being had. I have been willing to jump in and rescue the situation on their behalf, even if I have been the quiet one in the group myself.

We all have this rescuing potential within us and bring this to our human lives from our Prior Life experience, where we all offer best wishes and support to each other in The Room. If we can all stand up to the bully and be a rescuer when someone is in need, it will benefit both the rescued person and the rescuer. It does not mean that we jump in non-stop with all situations, but you will be able to sense when the time is right. This also does not mean that people should move into a victim role and always want to be rescued—if you can rescue *yourself* this is more satisfying, and moving into the victim role may mean that you are creating a problem to enable yourself to live in this role, and this is not good for either your emotional or physical health.

We can all be rescuers for family members and friends at some stage of our lives. We can also be rescuers for anyone in our society. Using your intuition will allow you to sense and know when to be a rescuer.

Fun And Excitement

This is an area of our lives that should be higher on the list than a lot of people realize. When we are born we have come from The Room, and we have a great excitement about our human life ahead. As young children we possess this fun and exciting side of us, and enjoy playing and trying new and different things. As we get older we start to become socialized and become a bit more aware of the perception of other people. As we get older still we take on more responsibilities, and our fun and excitement—once central to our life—may diminish to hobbies that can only be accommodated during vacations or free time. We may start to find that our sense of fun and excitement needs to be fuelled by alcohol and is only available to us after work or on weekends. This is not how it has to be. Fun and excitement is a natural element of both our psychology and our physiology, and we should be able to excel in it without always having to rely on a substance to release it.

Fun and excitement can happen at any time—remember they did when we were children. We need to find our inner child again and allow it out to play sometimes. We need to give our inner child a free rein and allow that fun to come out and find expression. Fun and excitement can mean different things to different people, but whatever it means to you, you should embrace it the way you did as a child.

They say that laughter is the best medicine, and I certainly believe that laughter, together with positivity and good energy, are a cocktail of happiness that cannot be beaten. I used fun quite often when I was working as a Youth Worker and saw that it worked with a lot of young people. I enjoy having lots of laughs with my friends and a good belly-aching laugh works wonders for picking up energy.

I am not saying that we should all just sit around telling jokes all day, but sometimes it almost feels like fun and excitement have a time and place and can only be used sparingly at those set times. Fun and excitement are important elements of our lives—and indeed our energies—and this should not be forgotten or underestimated. Release your inner child sometimes, and have fun and enjoy the excitement no matter what other people may think.

We are on Earth as part of an experience in the growth of our energy spirit, our soul. Make sure that you enjoy experiences; take on those that you can and those that you enjoy. I am not saying go on every roller coaster ride that you see just for the experience—especially if you hate roller coasters. What I am saying is that if you want to go to a particular country, make it a personal goal to do so. If there is a particular experience that you would like to do, say for example hot air ballooning, go ahead and try it. Remember that even a once in a lifetime experience can never be taken away from you—it is all a step on your personal journey. When you have completed an experience and have another one in mind, aim for that one. This life is an experience for our spirit energy, so each experience taken within this life is of benefit to our spirit energy. Fun and excitement are part of that experience, and we should make sure we participate in these more. Without them, life would be pretty gloomy.

A person without a sense of humor is like a wagon without springs. It's jolted by every pebble on the road. —Henry Ward Beecher

Forgiveness

This is an interesting one because forgiveness does not actually exist in The Room—for of course there is nothing to forgive. There are no judgments nor hostility towards one another, so forgiveness would not be a word included in a Prior Life dictionary. The reason I have put it here is that

The Room shows the importance of forgiveness from our human-life perspective. Even though we may not have anything to forgive in The Room, we know that it is a great feeling to not have this type of baggage attached to us, and we can continue with that feeling here on Earth.

I admit to not being the greatest teacher of forgiveness. Going back to when I was a small child—probably to before eight years old—forgiveness was a bigger part of my life. If a friend and I argued I could forgive, even if it was the other person's fault, as the friendship meant more to me than the argument. If I was unfairly told off by a teacher at school, I could forgive that. If my pets scratched me I could forgive them. You see, at that age and that stage in my life, I understood my Prior Life experience and The Room much more clearly. Forgiveness felt so natural because why would we want to carry around a burden and hold a degree of anger towards another person. That in-The-Room feeling was calling and it felt so good; why would I want to keep any resentment with me?

As I got older and become more humanized I forgave less and admit that forgiving became harder and harder. In fact, through late teenage years through to adulthood, revenge reared its ugly head more often than forgiveness. This, on occasion, brought out revenge's nasty cousin, *anger*. I have learnt that housing revenge and anger in one's life is not good for the body and soul. At forty-four years old, I am realizing again that forgiveness is the key to lightening the load of past burdens. Why carry unnecessary baggage around? I do not need to carry six backpacks full of burdens that are weighing me down and making me walk with a stoop. I can forgive, leave these backpacks behind, and walk upright and strong. I can be happy in the knowledge that forgiveness has allowed me to move on, unencumbered and without recourse.

I have started thinking about different points in my life where I have not forgiven people, and I am working on allowing this forgiveness to come through. One of the toughest times I have had to forgive involved a family member— a reaction and something said when we lost our baby to a miscarriage. This was obviously a very turbulent time in our lives, and the words and actions from this family member did not rest well with me. I carried around this hate for what they had said and done for many years, thinking that it was keeping me close to my baby and making me right in this situation. I have since learnt that, whether or not I was right or wrong in that situation, the unforgiving energy that I was sending out was not of any benefit to anyone, and it was actually of a major hindrance to me. When I finally forgave this person, I did feel a sense of release and now realize that it was better for me to let this hate go and forgive this person. I feel that forgiving this person has shown me that I can forgive anyone. You do not have to physically be in the same room or vicinity to forgive someone, just know that you are forgiving them within your heart.

It is an ongoing process and one that I have not completely mastered, but I know that as I move back into the way of living and thinking about forgiveness—the way I was as a child—forgiveness will flow naturally once more. A quote that I have thought of and told some people is *"when you release forgiveness, forgiveness releases you."* Just think about that for a moment. Work towards releasing forgiveness unto other people, and allow the forgiveness to release the extra baggage that is weighing you down.

> *He who seeks vengeance must dig two graves: one for his enemy and one for himself.* —Chinese Proverb

Release

As well as forgiving others we need to release emotions, and by emotions I am talking about the negative ones. Negative emotions wear away on us, and there is no point whatsoever in carrying them around. Earlier this year I had a ruptured appendix and had to go to hospital to have it removed. While I was in hospital, I ended up not being able to eat for a week due to *Physiological Ileus*, where the stomach does not work for a few days after an operation. During this time I was also vomiting up a lot of bile. When I look back on that time now, I feel that I gave myself a natural body detox and cleanse. The ruptured appendix was all my worries, concerns and negative emotions building up inside of me, and the week of not eating enabled my body to rid itself of toxins and poisons. As much as I would not want to go through what was a painful week in my life again, in some respects I think that this experience cleansed some of the negatives from me and has assisted in helping me grow my positive emotions, and I know that this is a lot better for my life ahead.

I know that, when I forgive someone, I feel a strong sense of release. I also know that, when I stop being bitter towards a particular person, time or event in my life, the release sensation is quite therapeutic for me. It is an exhilarating feeling to be able to release and move on with our lives and leave any negative baggage behind. It is a huge weight off of our shoulders. When you release something, you allow space for something else, so release the negativity and allow the positivity instead.

Alignment

Staying aligned with one's self is the key to keeping our beliefs, desires, teachings, learnings, and way of being on the path that we have chosen. There are ways that my wife and I keep ourselves and each other in alignment. We meditate every day and connect with our inner being, our highest self, our source, our spirit energy. With meditation, we can ask questions, find answers, and reaffirm the way we are living.

We also exercise together—this can be every day or not depending on what is going on in our lives at the time. The way we see it is that some exercise is better than no exercise. We have a fitness program, hike, and practice yoga.

We are a part of each other's support network and keep each other in check—and by this I mean that sometimes our humanized selves or egos can push through and we may not always notice it. Having someone to just gently point this out enables the other person to take stock of their thoughts and behaviour and reconnect with the true self. It can help us see what we are doing and help us on the right path ahead.

We share love. As I mentioned earlier, love is a very important aspect. It is the main ingredient of our soul, so having someone to share that love with is powerful. We share love with each other, our children, our family, our friends, society, strangers and nature—basically anything on which we can focus in a loving way. It does not mean you have to tell the person or physically be in the same place as them. Sharing love is a natural thing that we all do in The Room—and we can all do here on Earth.

I live in a friendly Universe that will support anything or desire that is aligned with the Universal Source of all. —Dr. Wayne Dyer

Trust The Process

When I was studying to be a counsellor, one of my teachers was a particularly wonderful warm person named Sally-Ann. She is a spiritual person who also runs retreats and workshops in the UK. I have learnt some tremendous teachings from Sally-Ann—both spiritually and vocationally. Something that has stuck in my mind over the years is something she often used to tell me: *trust the process*. Coming from The Room, we all trust the process by knowing that time, space, and the circumstance of our birth are all perfectly aligned. There have been times when trusting the process would have relieved stress and made my life easier. There have also been times where trusting the process has been beneficial to me.

When I was studying for my counselling diploma, I trusted the process. To receive my diploma meant three years of part-time studying. The first year was made up of two modules that each lasted six months and both modules had to be completed before moving on to the second year of studying. The second year was a full year of pure studying. The third year was a full year of studying with counselling placements and supervision—plus submit to personal counselling. Included within this were lots of essays, coursework and homework to complete. For the placements, I had to complete over one hundred hours of written counselling hours and receive the adequate supervision, which was one hour of supervision for every six hours of counselling work. For my own counselling, I had to have thirty hours of my personal counselling to unload any issues which may have been with me, and to experience how it feels to be a client on the other side of the counselling relationship. During this time I was also working and raising a family, so time was tight.

I know that some people had their reservations. They wondered that I would be able to complete the course and some had doubts that I had the ability to do it, even beyond the fact that I had to work and look after our family. Yet from the first time I set foot in the college I *knew* that I would complete it and that everything would be okay. The first two years were at our local college, but for the last year I had to go to a college in London—which was about two hours travel time each way from where I lived—to complete the counselling diploma. Even with all this, I never lost the faith, and I continued trusting the process. Time-wise everything seemed to fall into place, and I felt both honoured by the opportunity and proud of my achievements when I received my counselling diploma. I trusted the process. I *knew* and I succeeded! When my family and I immigrated to Canada, trusting the process could have saved me a great deal of grief. It was a very stressful time in our lives because it was not just a matter of deciding to move to Canada, packing our things, and moving there. There is an immigration process that we had to go through, and it took two years, and at no time was there any guarantee of success. Our dreams were on hold pending a final decision. During this time we had to continue with our lives, hoping for a positive outcome. I confess that my wife was better at handling the situation than I was, and she told me to *trust the process* a few times—I had told her about Sally-Ann and her advice already. As our application drew closer and closer to completion, more and more things fell into place for us. The exchange rate from British pounds to Canadian dollars went up, meaning we would have more money. The housing market picked up in the UK, which meant our house was worth more and would be quicker and easier to sell. We sold the possessions that we were not taking with us, and a friend bought our car and said we could have it until the day before we left, which meant that we would not have to rent one for our last couple of weeks in the UK. On the Canadian side, we moved just before the housing market picked up here, which meant we got our house cheaper and were able to watch it rise in value. After we had been in Canada for a few months, my wife said that I should have just trusted the process, and I had to agree with her that she was right and that this had been a good lesson for me.

I still have to put trusting the process into practice sometimes, but now I am a lot better at doing so. Sometimes I need to be reminded by my wife, and sometimes I can quickly remember it myself, but trusting the process is becoming easier for me again. I am currently trusting the process in writing this book.

All of these valuable lessons from The Room are important for us to comprehend because, if we can move away from the humanized negative emotions and put the positive in-The-Room knowledge and insights into our everyday lives, the world can progress in a more natural way to our true being. We have this truly amazing place where we come from—and return back to—so why not replicate it as much as we can in our human lives here on this Earth.

CHAPTER 4

We Are All Differently The Same

WHEN I WAS THINKING OF A TITLE FOR THIS BOOK, I WAS TRYING to be specific and wanted a title that portrays the messages within this book. I first thought about making the title *In Spirit,* but I noticed that there are a few books with spirit in their titles, and I did not want it to be mistaken for having any religious connotations as that is not the message that this book is sharing with you. I then moved on to *In 3, 2, 1… You're Back In The Room.* This title struck me as pretty catchy, but after consulting with my wife, we decided that people may not understand the title, and it is not showing the full picture of what this book is about. After this I thought about using *Prior Life,* but thought that this might give the impression that the book is about a past life rather than my Prior Life experience. *The Room* followed next, and this was high on the list, after all, the experiences, insights, experiences and knowledge written in this book is from The Room, but it still was not quite one hundred percent what I was looking for in a title. I thought about *World Changer,* but this can be from many different areas of life, so I moved on again. The next title that came to mind was *Heaven*—and The Room could be understood as being Heaven—but again I did not want this to become about religion, and even though the human description of heaven may match my description of The Room in some ways, I know this place as The Room and have always done so. For these reasons I passed on that particular title. I thought about it some more, and after discussing it with my wife, we thought about *The Missing Link*. This was also quite high on my list of titles, but in the end I decided that it was not fully describing what I wanted it to. All of these could have been used for the title, but I wanted a title that spoke about my Prior Life experience and time in The Room, and one which would really resonate with people. After more discussion we decided on the current title: *We Are All Differently The Same*. This title portrays exactly what I want to show in this book and passes out the loving messages of acceptance and connection; it explains that, upon leaving this planet at the end of our human lives, we shall all return and be the same once more in The Room. It shows, for all concerned, that dying here on Earth is not the end. Making this the title was easy in the end, and I feel it explains the content of this book perfectly. I have used some of the suggested titles as sub-headers in this book, for I feel that they still speak to aspects of the message. I also decided to give the title of this book its own chapter because its message is a particularly strong one. Please enjoy this chapter and the message within it.

A major memory from my Prior Life experience in The Room is the sense that we are all the same. We are all connected, yet here on Earth we see ourselves as different. I call this being *Differently The Same*. When we are living our human lives, we see each other as different in a multitude of ways. It can be through different genders: being male or female. It can be through different ethnicities: being white, black, brown or yellow. It can be through different nationalities: being British, Canadian, American or Chinese. It can be through different body shapes: being tall, short, obese or thin. It can be through different personal abilities: being athletic or academic. It can be through different sexual orientations: being homosexual or heterosexual. It can be through this, it can be through that. It can be through anything we like if we want it to be. The list goes on and on and on—yet when we are in The Room, in our Prior Life, we are all the same.

We can change this if we want to. We choose how we feel about people. We choose how we view people. We choose how we talk about people. We choose how we want to understand people. We are in charge of our own thought patterns and what messages we give out energetically or orally. We can choose to be more inclusive. We can choose to be more connected.

Sometimes I feel that there is a fear separating one nationality from another or one race from another or one culture from another. It is a fear of not understanding history, customs, and traditions. It is a fear of not recognizing that it is okay to be different—as we are actually all the same: Differently The Same. Once we can understand this and recognize that understanding is a two-way street—or in some cases a complicated intersection—then we can be more accepting, understanding and connected here in our world.

Look at it in this way: There are many countries in our world, around two hundred different countries in fact. Within each country there are people. All people are human beings. All human beings are made of flesh, blood and bone. All human beings possess spirit energy— a soul. All spirit energy will go back to the same place again, regardless where on this Earth you are exiting from—they will all go back to The Room. They will all be accepted and connected in The

Room. They will all have another Prior Life experience. The reason we are all people is that we are the same. The reason people are all human beings is that we are all the same. The reason human beings are made from flesh, blood and bone is that we are all the same. The reason human beings all have spirit energy is because we are all the same. The reason all spirit energy returns to The Room and is accepted and connected is that we are all the same. The reason that all spirit energy will have another Prior Life experience is that we are all the same. We are all Differently The Same. We need to understand this on Earth in the same way as our spirit energies can understand it in The Room.

We all came from the same place; and we will all go back to the same place. It is a cycle. Once we understand this Prior Life knowledge, I believe the world will be a better place, and we as human beings can treat each other better regardless of our humanized perceived differences, for we will recognize that we are all the same and all connected. Once we truly understand this, then fear, resentment, misunderstanding, prejudices—in fact all negative emotions—will fly out of the window, and positive emotions like love, acceptance, and understanding can shine through.

As a family we decided to emigrate to Canada for a variety of different reasons, and one of the reasons that was high on our list is that Canada is a highly multi-cultural society. I enjoy learning about different nationalities and cultures; remember my wife is Danish, and I enjoy participating in some of her traditions. I have a big interest in the First Nations history and culture and have enjoyed learning about some of their beliefs. Canada is a large country, the second largest in the world, and is a *relatively new* country, with people moving here from many countries of the globe to make Canada their new home. There are many countries represented within

Canadian society. Again, we all may appear different to the human eye, but our in-The-Room knowledge shows us that we are all the same. We are all Differently The Same.

We Are All Energy

The energy that we portray to others can be read quite easily; it is a form of non-verbal communication. I would rather go and sit and talk to a calm, smiling, happy person who is relaxed and sending out a positive, glowing energy to the world than a scowling, angry looking person whose energy projects agitation and aggression. We are all energy, and we all use and pick up on different energy all the time. In fact all of nature does. Animals can sense good or bad energy. If you are at home and in a happy mood, your dog will pick up on it and happily wag its tail. If you are in an angry mood, your dog will be more distant and may not wag its tail quite so freely. It is the energy that the dog picks up in this scenario, and it is the energy that we all use in every scenario.

I'll give you an example. Imagine that you are at a farmer's market, and in a box on a table there are two apples: one is a good shiny, juicy-looking apple and the other is a bad, slimy, almost rotten apple. You ask the apple seller how much they are and are told that, as it is the end of the day, they are free and you are welcome to take one. They are both free, and so you take the good apple—after all why would you even bother with the bad apple? It's the same with energy. Energy is free, whether good energy or bad energy, the cost is the same. So why not choose the good energy? Why even bother with the bad energy? It's not like you are getting less energy choosing the good one. It's not as if the good energy is limited and needs to be used sparingly. It is as easy a choice to choose the good energy over the bad energy as it is choosing the good apple over the bad apple. I know in life there will be times when we have bad energy showing itself in certain situations—such as the loss of a loved one—but the sooner we can release that energy and move back into the good energy the more beneficial it will be.

The other thing about good and bad energy is that good energy can enable good results. Bad energy can enable bad results. Just think about this for a minute. How many wars were started because of good energy? How many crimes are committed because of good energy? In fact how much of *any* of the negativity in the World is created by good energy? Now think about this for a moment. How much money is raised for charitable organizations through good energy? How much love is shared in the world through good energy? How much awareness is promoted to good causes through good energy? Once again, when we think about good and bad energy in this context, the good energy is the clear winner every time. We are all energy, and when we left The Room, we were good energy. Let us continue to allow the good energy to shine through the way it does in The Room. Let us all choose good energy.

Perception

People's perception is a big issue with all of us—yes I am including myself in this, although I am already working on returning to my childlike—not childish—stance of not caring about other people's perception. You see, as a child and even a young adult, other people's perception did not bother me. That is why I could be a punk and not worry about what people thought. I could be the class clown and not worry about what other people thought. I could be the one willing to take on challenges, big or small, and still not worry about what other people thought. As I grew older, I became more aware of what other people thought and how I was perceived. Instead of being natural about certain aspects of my life, I moved into other people's perceptions. I went from caring more about what I wanted to do and what I wanted to look like and how I wanted to be, and I shifted in order to fit into other people's mould of how I should be. I realise this was a mistake.

As I grew into adulthood and became aware of responsibilities and societal rules, I took on the baggage of perception even more than before and continued to worry about what other people thought. I lived this way for a while before realizing that, at the end of the day, other people's perception doesn't matter. Working past other people's perception will enable you to live your life fuller. I have worked through a lot of this, but I know that I still have certain times when I may worry about what I am wearing or what people may think. I am teaching myself, through my own Prior Life experiences in The Room, that all perception is trivial and unimportant in the greater scheme of things. When we return to The Room, there will be no perceptions on us from others, and we will all be the same.

Our perceptions of other people are just as problematic, just as fraught with potential harm. We all need to be aware of our own perceptions of others and take responsibility for the potential consequences.

Image

One cannot discuss perception without discussing image. Our image is very important to us, and we want to project the best image of ourselves that we can. We can do this in a number of ways. We project a superficial image through how we dress. We can work to emulate the image of a particular role model. Or we can portray an image of congruence, a *genuine* image. I am not saying that looking smart is not a good image to have, but a genuine image is what we carry off best. If you are genuine in your image and show this to other people, they are able to see the real you. There will be nothing hidden and no secrets lurking. Anything that moves away from your genuine image is illusory. For instance, it may be that you want to project an edgy, bad boy image—maybe you want to be seen as *gangster*. Modern society has promoted and glamourized dark, dangerous personas often at the expense of clean honest ones which are diminished even demeaned. Think how many celebrities cloak themselves in these sorts of images. If we continue to show and support good as bad and bad as good, then we cannot really complain about the culture of crime, violence and drugs that flourishes as a result. The promotion of negative images over positive is at the very root of the uneasiness that some people feel about going out in certain places after dark.

I know from my own experience that, when I was younger, I felt good promoting the bad image because I was out living some of those things. I also recognize, now that I am older and look at things differently, how much I fooled myself by believing a pretend image of who I was instead of the true image. I have moved on, through my choices and decisions, and society can as well if it wants to. If we all make a stand, promoting a good, genuine image instead of the bad, false image, then we can all show our real selves and continue in the promotion of positivity in our everyday lives.

The image you display is from you and you alone. You choose your image. You are your image.

Every man builds his world in his own image. He has the power to choose, but no power to escape the necessity of choice. —Ayn Rand

Judgments, Stereotypes, Labels, And Boxes

We are all energy. We are all human beings, and we are all connected—yet humankind still likes to judge, stereotype, label and put people in boxes. Why do we feel the need to do this? I have never seen a herd of cows exclude a particular cow because it is of a different colour to the majority of the herd. All of these expressions are negative in the extreme, and ones that we can definitely do without in our society. If we say someone is *this* or someone is *that,* it can be difficult for us to remove them from that vision and reintegrate them. On the other hand, if we do not judge, stereotype, label or box in the first place, but instead accept people for who they are and befriend them, then it would be very difficult to segregate them later on. Acceptance fosters compassion, and compassion represents the power of positivity over negativity. Compassion means more peace in our lives and throughout the world.

I feel that political correctness has helped through the promotion of neutral non-judgmental language and the suppression of small forms of ubiquitous stereotyping. Used in the right way the PC movement will continue to do so. On the flip side, if it is used in the wrong way, it can have the opposite effect and almost turn people's opinions back to what they were—anything taken to an extreme becomes distorted and *Political Correctness gone mad* is no exception. We are all equal so let us all continue to act accordingly.

When we return to The Room we will all be the same. There will be no judgments There will be no stereotypes. There will be no labels or boxes. These are all human, worldly inventions that we should work on to eradicate from our lives so that we can live a more inclusive and connected existence here on Earth, similar to that in The Room.

> *A human being is part of a whole, called by us the universe, a part limited in time and space. He experiences himself, his thoughts and feelings, as something separated from the rest a kind of optical delusion of his consciousness. This delusion is a kind of prison for us, restricting us to our personal desires and to affection for a few persons nearest us. Our task must be to free ourselves from this prison by widening our circles of compassion to embrace all living creatures and the whole nature in its beauty.*
> —Albert Einstein

Acceptance And Connection

I originally ended this chapter with the Einstein quote you just read, but I have recently witnessed an experience that I really wanted to share with everyone in this book.

Yesterday my wife and I took the Danish visitors we have staying with us to our annual local Pow-Wow here in the Cowichan Valley on Vancouver Island. It was a beautiful sunny day, and the venue was the perfect setting for a nice day enjoying First Nations culture and traditions. Seeing the

First Nations men, women and children all dressed up in their fine regalia was very pleasing to both the eye and the heart. This was the first time that our visitors had ever been to a Pow-Wow, and they were really taken by the atmosphere and proceedings.

After we had been walking round and looking at the stalls for a while, an announcement was made for the Grass Dancers to be ready. We found a place to stand and watch, and we really enjoyed watching the young people dancing. I have always said that the drumming and singing that accompanies the dancing gives me goose bumps, and I once again found it very powerful indeed. After this was the Grand Parade, where all the dancers, from the very young all the way up to the Elders, came into the arena and danced and showed their Pow-Wow dance outfits and ceremonial wear. During this time we were not allowed to take any photos, but that was fine as it gave us more time to enjoy the parade.

One of our guests is a lady called Winnie; she is seventy-eight years old. She was the child minder of my wife, and my wife says she is like her second mother. Winnie does not look seventy-eight; in fact I did not know she was that old until my wife told me— she only looks about sixty. She is an inspiration to our family.

While the parade was going around, Winnie was swaying around to the drumming and the singing and said she would love to go out and dance. At the end of the Grand Parade everybody in the arena started to go round in a circle, dancing as they went, and I noticed some people were joining them from the audience. I went to ask one of the organizers if it was okay to take photos now, and he replied that it was okay and we could also join in the dancing for this section of the Pow-Wow if we wanted to. I went back, and my wife translated to Winnie—who only speaks Danish—that it was okay to join in and dance. Winnie did not need any more prompting than that and was soon out in the arena dancing around with all the First Nations dancers. She completed a lap, having fun dancing, and then came back to where we were standing.

A moment later something amazing happened. One of the First Nations Elders, who had been dancing behind Winnie, beckoned her out to join him. She went out, and he gave her some of his feathers that were in a fan to hold. He then proceeded to show her how to move her feet, and she was escorted around the arena for another lap with him as her chaperone. Remember Winnie does not speak any English, and this Elder does not speak any Danish, but between them they knew what the other person meant and they looked so fine dancing round together. After finishing that dance together, Winnie returned the feather fan to the elder and they bowed a goodbye to each other. Winnie returned to us once more and shared her delight with us for the fantastic experience she had just had.

This really struck a chord with me, for here were two people from different countries and cultures, who both had a common interest for a moment in time. They may not have been able to communicate verbally, but they still enjoyed sharing customs and traditions together. Winnie was over the moon with the experience, and I could see that the First Nations Elder was pleased that Winnie had shown an interest in his culture; he had been happy to share it with her. They had never met before, and they will probably never meet again. They definitely will never speak again because of the language barrier. Yet together they connected for two minutes of their lives and will stay connected together forever in the story that they share. I found this very inspiring to watch, and it showed me a great example of accepting and connecting with others. This one scenario gives a fantastic vision that we are all Differently The Same. I am very pleased to have shared this with you.

Chapter 5
Living As A Whole Person

This is probably going to be the shortest chapter in this book, but I wanted to make it a chapter rather than a sub-section because I feel that this is a very important issue.

When we think about who we are and what we can do, it can quite often come down to whether we are male or female. We see males one way and we see females another way—yet *should* we? We have ideas of what males can do and ideas of what females can do, but are those ideas realistic? There are traditional roles that we see for both males and females, but can those roles be reversed? When I was in The Room I did not see us as either male or female, only as spirit energy as a whole. In this chapter I will look at how we, as human beings, can live our lives as a whole person. What do I mean when I say *we can live our lives as a whole person*? Let me explain.

Male Roles

As a society we have particular roles that we feel are male roles. This can be seen in any town or city, up and down any country in the world. Male roles tend to be seen more traditionally as the provider/hunter/gatherer and they are expected to be able to complete more physically challenging tasks. When male babies are born a stereotypical image can be born with them: being a quarter back for an NFL team, a point guard in the NBA, or a racing driver for NASCAR. They are expected to play in the mud, hold frogs, and climb trees. They will be allowed a little more freedom when they are older and have a bit more leeway when they start out in their dating days. This is the human vision of males, it is what males do. Or is it?

What if that is not what a particular male wants to do? What if they do not want to play football, participate in basketball or race a car? How do we feel about that? What if they wanted to do something that has traditionally been seen as more for females than males?

I remember, when I was in the UK and my son was born, I said that he was a future soccer star in the making. Some friends of mine were trying to wind me up and have a laugh and asked how I would feel if he wanted to be a dancer instead. My reply was instant in coming. You see, I was not bothered and never *have been* bothered about what my children might choose to do in life. If my son grew up and hated soccer then I would not force him to play it just because of my love for The Beautiful Game. If he wanted to dance then it would have been fine for him to dance.

As it turned out my son did play soccer but also played basketball when we arrived in Canada. Due to a clash with training and game times he had to make a decision between soccer and basketball and chose basketball. As a parent, I took a backseat and allowed him to decide what sport he liked best and supported him in it once he had made his decision. I still have some people who ask me if I wish he had stuck with soccer—I am so passionate about soccer—but I always reply that it is his life, his decision and I am always proud watching him whatever he is doing.

In this example my son may have chosen one expected male role, a basketball player, over another expected male role, a soccer player, but it would not have mattered to me whatever he had chosen, whether it had been one with a traditional male role or not.

Female Roles

Society tends to see traditional female roles as the nurturer, the family-raiser, the homemaker. When female babies are born a stereotypical image can be born with them too: being a famous dancer, Olympic gymnast, or a top model. They are expected to play dress up, love ponies, and bake cakes. They will have a little more of a protective arm kept around them when they are older and will definitely have more of an eye on them when they start dating. This is the human vision of females; it is what females do. Or is it?

What if that is not what a particular female wants to do? What if they do not want to dance, do gymnastics, or be a model? How do we feel about that? What if they wanted to do something that has traditionally been seen as more for males than females?

I remember when my daughter was born and I saw her as a little dancer. At around three years old she wanted to dance, so we found a dance school nearby and signed her up for lessons. She did this for a while and then wanted to try gymnastics and we found a gymnastics class. She did this for a while and then wanted to try acting and we found a local acting group. She has also been a member of a couple of swimming clubs, tried her hand at judo, at soccer, at volleyball, at basketball and with some more drama groups. Yet throughout all these tries at different activities she has stuck with dance throughout. This is her passion and has stuck with her throughout the years.

In this example my daughter has enjoyed doing a traditional female role, but she has also been able to branch out and dip her feet in less traditional roles. Whether she had stuck with dancing or moved heavily into judo I would have supported her either way. Whatever her choice was would also be our choice. I will support her in whatever choices she makes.

Changes In Roles

Now, before everyone starts screaming that basketball and soccer are no longer just male roles and dancing and modelling are no longer just female roles, I will lead into what my point is. I am pleased that barriers in these sports—and indeed many others—have been broken. When I was a teenager at high school, going back about thirty years now, males played soccer, rugby, basketball and cricket, and females did field hockey, netball, dance and volleyball with both sexes having athletic teams. In just thirty short years, barriers have been broken and knocked down to allow either sex to participate in each other's sports. Here in Canada women's soccer teams are very good, and it does not surprise me seeing how many girls play soccer every week. Growing up in the UK girls soccer was not promoted, and women's soccer teams were almost a novelty. Why was that? In school I only played volleyball and hockey a couple of times, and my friend had to ask permission to play volleyball because he was a boy, yet men's volleyball is big here in North America, and the male players are very good.

The way that sports are breaking the barriers to male and female roles is a start, but there are plenty of more ways barriers can come down and inclusion for all can be accepted. There are still areas in our lives where we can be more allowing of changing roles. When we do, we can live more as a whole person, enjoying whatever role we want regardless of historical precedents.

In The Room there is no traditional male role, we are allowed to just *be*. Whatever role your son, male friend, husband, boyfriend, father or any other significant male chooses to do please accept and respect their decision. In The Room there is no traditional female role either. Whatever role your daughter, female friend, wife, girlfriend, mother or any other significant female chooses to do, please accept and respect their decision. Please also accept and respect the roles any other person chooses to take. Please allow them to be the whole person.

Males Allowing Their Feminine Side Out

When I was born and grew up as a young boy, it was not very common for men to change diapers or feed the baby. Men were not expected to cook, and helping with the housework was only in an emergency in our house. Jobs were gender-specific and that was how it was, end of story! Move forward a few years, and I enjoyed being the doting father to my children, even at diaper-changing time. At school I did not particularly like needlework even though we had to take it for one term, but I did quite enjoy cooking and looked forward to the term. Nowadays I still do not sew, I probably haven't since that last lesson back in school, but I still enjoy cooking. I like thinking about what to make, buying the ingredients from the store and making the finished plate, the whole deal. I help with the housework, do the laundry and vacuum. I am so happy that I helped raise my children from birth to adulthood. I also worked in a heavily female orientated career when I was counselling and loved my job. And the best bit is I allowed myself to do so!

Females Allowing Their Masculine Sides Out

Back in my school days, girls did needlework and cooking as standard, and although they did participate in the metalwork and woodwork lessons, it was unusual for girls to pursue it further. When I was in construction, I remember seeing my first female truck driver and my first female engineer. Nowadays there are many females involved in the construction industry in various jobs, and this is great to see. Women are not expected to just stay at home and be the housewife. More and more couples are doing roles together now and breaking the role expectations altogether, and this includes things like dangerous sports or home DIY.

The Whole You Living Your Life

So why did I write this chapter? There are a couple of reasons that I feel are very important. The first reason is that a lot of the roles I have mentioned have changed over the years for the better. This can still be improved to equal numbers, but the changes in some of these roles is already quite large— although these are not the only ones in which changes are needed. What I am trying to show is that change is possible and people are able to live their lives in whatever style or manner they desire. If you want to live a particular way, but your role doesn't traditionally fit that, so what? It is your life, live your whole life and live it to the fullest.

Another reason why all this is important is that, if we can change our thoughts and opinions and accept role changes, we then accept the people doing so. If we learn to accept the fact that some people are changing the norm, we will learn to accept more people and eventually all people regardless of the biases formed against them.

When we are having our Prior Life experience there are no rules, no particular masculine side, no particular feminine side, just spirit energies all connecting and combining for the greater good of all. If we can bring that to Earth with us, we can promote that same greater good approach here every day in our lives. We have to accept others as they are and be happy for who they are. We have to allow ourselves to be who we want to be and be happy for ourselves.

Breaking The Mould

In conclusion, I want to show that, with the correct input and allowing from all of our behalves, we can break the mould of certain beliefs. We can live a whole life and allow others to live a whole life too, however we or they choose to live, regardless of roles. Just because something is a certain way or is seen in a particular way does not mean that it has to be that way forever. It is not good to have things set in stone—that does not allow growth both personally and soci-etally. By breaking through these traditional male and female roles we succeed in breaking the mould as well.

Male and female represent the two sides of the great radical dualism. But in fact they are perpetually passing into one another. Fluid hardens to solid, solid rushes to fluid. There is no wholly masculine man, no purely feminine woman. —Margaret Fuller

CHAPTER 6

Intuitiveness

AS A YOUNG CHILD, I WAS QUITE INTUITIVE. I WOULD SOMETIMES know things that were going to happen. As I got older and discarded some of my knowledge from The Room, my intuitiveness also decreased. Something that has always stuck in my mind from this period of my life involved meeting people—perhaps just walking along in the street—and knowing that I had *seen* the person before. Sometimes they were children my age, and sometimes they were adults, and I just knew that I had seen them before. Sometimes I would say hello or smile at them or make eye contact—I can remember being rebuffed by them and not understanding why. Once I became humanized, I did not do this so often, even if I had the same intuitive *I know you* thoughts about a person. I now understand that I did know them, not from our human existence, but from The Room. You see, in The Room, we communicate non-verbally, in a kind of telepathic, intuitive way. We know, encourage and support each other. The strong feelings of *I know you* were because I recognized the spirit energy from The Room, rather than the human being who they had been transformed into. I know, as a child, I would find it strange that these people I tried to communicate with would not acknowledge me, but I now know why. I know

I recognized them but they did not recognize me because they did not remember their experience of Prior Life in The Room. I also think that is why babies can stare, smile and coo at certain people they may not have seen before—they are still remembering them from The Room. If you ever find yourself walking down a street and you see someone and think *I know them from somewhere*, perhaps you do, although not from here on Earth; perhaps you know them from your own Prior Life experience.

My intuitiveness has never been as strong as it was when I was a young child, but there have been times in my life when I have had intuitive feelings about something and acted on them and been rewarded with a positive outcome. I can also give an examples of how not fully listening to my intuition have resulted in not-so-good outcomes. When I was playing soccer I was not the fastest player on the soccer pitch but could rely on my skills, sliding tackles, and my secret weapon, my *intuition*. You see I was quite often in the right place at the right time or even ahead of time. It was as if I had this sense of where the ball would go before either my teammates or opposing players even kicked it. What I lacked in speed, I certainly made up for in intuition. I can distinctly remember one time when I went ignored my intuition and it cost me the chance to score a goal and possibly win the game for my team.

A teammate of mine was battling for the ball, and I knew *intuitively* where I should stand, without being marked by any opposition players, knowing the ball would come to me. All I would have to do is turn and shoot the ball, and I would have a really good chance of scoring from where I was standing. Unfortunately, my teammate took longer winning the ball than I anticipated, and because I played as a defender, I thought I better get back into defence in case he did not

win the ball. As soon as I started running back, my teammate
did win the ball and played it to the exact place where I had
been standing seconds before.

Without me being there to turn and shoot towards goal,
the ball just ran harmlessly to one of the opponent's defend-
ers who was able to clear the ball away easily—we ended up
drawing the game with this team. I still mull that one over
in my mind; if I had continued listening to my intuition we
could have won the game. Out of many games of soccer I
have played over the years, this one incident in this particular
game has always stuck in my mind as a lesson to me not to
doubt my intuition. Like all of us, I am still working on it.

This next example dates back to the time that I had
booked my place on the first term of my counselling course.
At the time, we did not have much money so trying to find
the extra funds to pay for the course was a struggle. One
night I had a dream that a Formula One racing driver called
Eddie Irvine won his first Grand Prix. I woke up and told
my wife about it, and we agreed that we should act on it
if I ever recognize the race track on television. I was a big
fan of Formula One racing, and I used to watch as many
qualifying sessions and races as I could. I was watching the
Formula One qualifying session a few weeks later for the
Australian Grand Prix. There, right in front of me, was the
exact same track that I had dreamt about. My wife and I
decided to scrape together some money and put a bet on
Eddie Irvine to win the race. The next day Eddie won the
Australian Grand Prix—his first Formula One racing win—
and I won enough money to pay for my first term at college.
Intuitiveness, premonition, sixth sense, gut feeling, whatever
you like to call it, if I feel strongly enough about something, I
will act out on it or look for it in the future.

Intuition With Nature

Have you ever had moments where, without saying anything to your pet as they lay on the floor, you think a thought about them and they suddenly look up at you as though reading your mind? That's intuition with nature. A form of communicating without the need for speech or gesture. I have had this happen myself with domestic pets, wild animals, and insects.

Animals do it all the time. For example, we have two dogs and two cats and they all get along fine. One of our cats does not like other dogs barking but is fine with the two he knows. If he is outside and another dog barks he will instantly run inside the house as fast as he can. Yet if our dogs bark he will stay outside as he intuitively knows that he is safe with them. I can think of times where I have communicated my thoughts to be advantageous to both me and pets, wild animals and insects, and I would like to share some examples of this with you.

With Domesticated Animals And Pets

The first example involves a domesticated rabbit called Floppy. The previous owners of the house we live in now emigrated to Costa Rica and asked us if we would adopt Floppy. We agreed, and for the first few months Floppy the Rabbit was happy living in his large pen. A short time later we got some Guinea Pigs and put them in the same run as Floppy, and they all got along really nicely. For a while this worked well but after a couple of months Floppy had chewed through the wire and escaped. A neighbour from up our road found Floppy and put a sign up saying 'Rabbit Found'.

We went and claimed Floppy and brought him back home. The wire was duly fixed, and Floppy was put back in his pen again. After about a week Floppy escaped again, and this time I caught him in our garden. Once more the wire was fixed and once more Floppy was reinstated in his home. Less than a week later Floppy escaped for a third time and my wife and I decided that Floppy obviously did not want to be caged up, and if we or any one else found him we would let him run free and take his chances with the other Canadian wildlife. Our next door neighbour came by later that day with Floppy in the back of his truck, so we told him about our plan to let Floppy live wild and that if our neighbour ever saw him out he would know it was okay. I picked up Floppy from the back of our neighbours truck and carried him to the side yard near where his pen was. Instantly, poor Floppy had this look of dread that he would be put back into his pen again. I held Floppy and told him that if he stayed close by I would let him have his freedom. Then I bent down and put him on the ground. I have never seen a rabbit so happy and excited. He ran round and round my feet and I could tell he had understood the message I had given him. Floppy stayed near our house and a couple of neighbours yards for about a year, living as a wild rabbit, and he even had another rabbit friend that he hung around with quite often. If I was out working in our field or blackberry picking, Floppy would quite often hop out of the hedge and come and say hello and he would still let me stroke him. He once stayed with me nearly all day while I was planting garlic. Floppy was not seen again after about a year and neither was his other rabbit friend. We are not sure if they were taken by other people who thought they were escaped pets, went the way of nature or something else, but I am so pleased that I was able to give Floppy the Rabbit his wish of living like a real wild rabbit, knowing he understood that it was okay to do so. It made me happy that Floppy was happy, and that's all that either one of us could have asked for.

With Wild Animals

Another example involves a stag that we have called Prince. We have known Prince since he was a young orphan deer. One of the reasons we bought our home is because it has three and a half acres of land, and we could enjoy the privacy, the quiet and the nature that surrounds us. One evening me, my wife and our son were sitting outside talking, when all of a sudden a very young deer came from behind a tent we had set up in the garden and started eating the grass very close to us. It was summer and the grass here turns brown and crispy quite quickly in the sun, and this poor young deer was struggling to find much to eat. By this stage he had got within about six feet of where we were sitting. We could tell that he was nervous of us, but at the same time he was hungry and was willing to take the risk of getting close to us. We could see he was really small, and normally the fawns are still with their mother at this age, but there was no mother in sight. We all reassured this young deer, as best we could, that it was okay and he could stay around and we got some apples from inside our house and gave them to him. He devoured them in a short time and we found other fruit and vegetables for him as well. He stayed around in our field for a couple of months and would sometimes venture into the forest at the end of our field, but always came back to our field to sleep. When he was a bit older we could tell he was a stag, for he had a couple of small bumps appearing on his head—that's when we named him Prince. Over the rest of the year, Prince grew into quite the young stag, and he was now venturing further out and spending less time in our field, until it got to the stage where he was gone for what we thought was forever, but since then Prince has come back every year to see us and show off his antlers. Although we could never get right up to him—even as an orphan—we can still get pretty close and I still have little chats with him. Last year Prince came and hung around in our field for a few days just as he had in the past, and I am looking forward to his visit again this year.

With Insects

Like most people I am not a big fan of wasps. I am not scared of them—although as a boy aged twelve I did accidentally disturb a wasp nest and got stung many times on that occasion. From then on I decided that they could only sting me, and I began to lose any fear of them. Since that incident as a twelve-year-old, I have been stung again but it no longer fazes me nor makes me fear wasps, and I am quite comfortable knocking down wasps nests when need be. This story involves some wasps that were living in behind the siding of my barn, right by the door that I had to unlock to get at my mower and garden tools. As I have said before, knocking down wasp nests and moving the wasps on does not bother me, but this nest was in an awkward position right behind the plywood panel. Every time I unlocked the padlock on the barn door, at least three or four wasps would fly out and I would have to whack them to be able to unlock the door and get it open. This went on for the best part of a week with neither me nor the wasps being a clear winner, and both of us being frustrated with the other. Finally I said to the wasps, "If you stop trying to fly at me and sting me every time I come and unlock this door, I won't disturb you and you can nest here for this summer only. "

From that moment onwards, whenever I went to the barn door to unlock it, about two or three wasps would come out and stand by the nest entrance on the paneling but not fly towards me. This would happen every time I went to unlock the barn door for the rest of the summer. They gained a safe and secure spot for their nest, and I had easy access to my barn without having to worry about swatting wasps each time. A win–win situation that was communicated in a way that many other people would say could not be done with nature. At the end of the summer, once the wasps had gone, I raked out the nest as best I could with a pruning saw to deter them coming back.

I am currently doing the same with some wasps that are nesting on a flower pot in our garden—my message to these particular wasps this year is this; keep away from the house and you can stay for this summer. So far I have not had to worry about any wasps, from their nest, trying to sting me in the garden.

I wrote about this second experience with the wasps nesting on a flower pot a couple of days ago but feel that I have to add this after what happened today. We have some family staying with us from Europe and they very kindly offered to do a bit of gardening for us. In the evening I was out in the garden with them and noticed that they were poking things around this particular flower pot where the wasps were. I asked what they were doing and they said in fearful voices, "Careful, there is a wasps nest there. " I then remembered I had not told them about the agreement I had with these wasps. I moved the objects that they were putting around the nests and sure enough the wasps were looking agitated and angry. I communicated with the wasps that all was okay, that I am a man of my word, and they could still stay for the summer, and the wasps settled down again. I was able to move the objects away from the nest without the wasps being antagonized—in fact they seemed relieved to see me! While I was doing this my guests had moved away shouting, "Watch out, you'll get stung. " I think they were taken aback that the wasps settled back down without any stinging incidents taking place. Afterwards I explained to my visitors the agreement that I had with these particular wasps and they looked at me a little strange, not really understanding why I would want to save wasps, who are a pest after all. It does not mean I will save every wasps nest I see either. In fact this year I have already knocked down a few different wasps nests that were on my house and garage and continue to do so if they nest where I do not want them to be.

For me it is more about the intuitive communication I have had with these wasps on two occasions, where they have become calm and even allowed me to do gardening and be quite close to their nest, without any threat to either of us.

So you can see from these examples that we can communicate intuitively and have these strong and powerful connections, with domestic pets, wild animals and insects. We communicate this way with each other in The Room. When we are in The Room we understand that we are all connected. We need to understand we are all connected here on Earth.

The reason that I have written about this intuitiveness with nature is that we all have this intuitive feeling and connection with others, but we do not always use it. If we know we have this intuitive way with domestic pets for example—and many times I have heard people say that they can get their pets' attention without talking to them—then we can learn how to use it with each other. I am working very hard on improving my own intuition, for I realize how valuable a tool it can be in my life and I encourage you to do the same.

CHAPTER 7

The Law Of Attraction

THE LAW OF ATTRACTION IS A NICE FOLLOWUP TO INTUITIVENESS for both speak to our innate connectedness to the world around us.

In a nutshell, the Law of Attraction suggests that whatever you *think* about you *bring* about—both positively and negatively. It is about the manifestation of desires, and why therefore it is important that you manifest positive desires. The Law of Attraction is something that I have used over the years without really knowing it, and something that I have used in recent years with a definite emphasis on manifesting positive outcomes. I have read the book *The Law of Attraction* by Esther & Jerry Hicks and also the book (of the same name) by Michael Losier, and they are very useful for anyone who wishes to understand or learn more about the Law of Attraction. I would definitely recommend both books.

I would like to share a couple of instances where I have used the Law of Attraction for positive outcomes. The first example is with one of our dogs. My daughter and I were looking for another dog, and we had been looking at the Goldendoodle breed of dog—Golden Retriever–Poodle mixes—but they were in the eight hundred to twelve hundred dollar range, which was more money than we had available to spend. I put out into the Universe my rockets of desire that I would like a Goldendoodle puppy for less than three hundred dollars. We carried on checking online adverts, breeders and kennels and within three days of putting out my desire, we found an advert for a kennel who were doing their annual three puppy give away. Basically the kennel mentioned, donated the proceeds of three puppies annually to a charity. What we had to do was apply for one of the available puppies and, if we were chosen, we had to donate two hundred dollars to the charity of the kennel's choice and pay a fifty dollar delivery fee to have the puppy flown in to where we lived on Vancouver Island. I emailed the kennel with the information that they were asking for including details about our family, the pets we already had and our experience with dogs. A couple of days later I received an email stating that we were one of the families chosen and within four days after that our new puppy Charlie was laying on his new bed in our house. Our total expenditure was less than three hundred dollars, exactly as I had asked the Universe for with my rockets of desire.

Another example that comes to mind involves a contest our local radio station ran last year: the prize was a four-night trip to Las Vegas, complete with limousine to and from the airport, vouchers for clothes, five hundred dollars spending money, sunglasses and suitcases. My daughter entered my name into the contest, and the radio station called me to let me know I was one of the seventy-five people chosen to go forward to the final stage. Once I found out I had made it through to the finale, I deliberately put the Law of Attraction into action by visualizing myself winning the trip and how I would celebrate my win.

The finale night came, and we went to where the competition was being held. The winner would be decided through elimination bingo: all the contestants were given a number from a bingo card and the bingo machine fired up. If your number was chosen, you were out of the competition—the last person standing would be the winner. As I said I had already visualized myself winning, but all through the contest I kept focused on my number not being picked; my number was B8.

They started the bingo machine and began drawing balls out. One by one other contestants began to drop out of the competition as their bingo numbers were chosen. I made it to the last fifty. More numbers were drawn and more people exited from the competition. I made it to the last twenty. I concentrated on my number not being drawn. I made it to the last ten. I remembered how I would celebrate the win I was going to have. I made it to the last five and now the last five of us left in the contest were invited up to the front of the hall. As I stood there my focus was simply on my number not being chosen, I KNEW I was going to win. I made it to the final two and waited for the final number to be drawn. I was one number away from claiming my prize to Las Vegas. The last number came out the machine and it was not mine, I had won! I did my celebration exactly as I had envisioned it, gave my wife a big hug and participated in the radio interview for the radio station. I had put out my rockets of desire into the Universe to win this trip to Las Vegas; I had allowed this prize to come to me exactly as I had forecast it, and I knew that I would win. The perfect ending and Law of Attraction result for me. Oh, and we had a great time in Las Vegas, baby!

Both of these examples show how putting out desires into the Universe can work through manifesting. It's the Law of Attraction in action. Send out your rockets of desire, and reap the results.

It is interesting how many people call you lucky if you use the Law of Attraction to manifest your desires. Even with the example of winning the Las Vegas trip and telling people beforehand that I knew I was going to win, some people still said, "Darren, you are always lucky. "When I try to explain the Law of Attraction and say that I had already told them that I would win, they do not take this into account: "It's because you are lucky. " Either that or I hear, "Lucky you, I would *never* win a trip like that. " I can honestly answer that you will not win a trip like that if that is the message you are sending out into the Universe. Send out positive rockets of desire to manifest for your Law of Attraction.

Allowing

Allowing is an important part of the Law of Attraction. Without allowing, the rockets of desire that you may be sending out cannot manifest the desire. I always think of allowing as the tricky part of the Law of Attraction, because you can think of what it is you want to manifest and you can send out your rockets of desire to get it, but allowing can be difficult. Sometimes we send out our desires but then have little niggling doubts about what we have asked for, and this can stop the allowing. Sometimes we want something, but after sending out our desires do not want to wait for it, so this can stop the allowing. Sometimes the desire we have asked for seems too big and impossible or too little and insignificant, so this can stop the allowing. Allowing is sending out your desires to the Universe and *believing* that they will manifest. Knowing that what you asked for—whatever the size of the desire—is possible. Knowing that it will manifest for you at the exact time scale you require it. If you can learn to allow manifesting, your desires will be an easier concept for you.

I am not always the best at allowing but, like everything I am writing about in this book, I am working at getting better at it. The more I work at it, the better it gets. In The Room we allow and we are born at the perfect time for what we want in this life. Allow yourself to allow.

The Command

I have spoken about intuitiveness and the Law of Attraction and one more aspect of these which is slightly more forceful is the Command. I have used this in my life before, again without necessarily knowing it at the time, and it has brought me positive outcomes. An example I would like to share with you here happened to me earlier this year and is still very fresh in my mind.

At the beginning of April, I was taken into hospital with appendicitis. My appendix actually ruptured around 10 pm that evening in the hospital, and I was told that I would have it removed the next morning. The surgeon came and saw me the next day, and said I would probably only be in for one night as the operation is performed by laparoscopic surgery. I had the operation and the appendix was removed. I returned to the ward to recover and waited for the following day to arrive, expecting to go home. Unfortunately, my stomach stopped working due to the surgery, a condition called *Physiological Ileus*, which meant that any fluids that I was having—I was not allowed solids—would not go through my stomach and I would have intense vomiting of bile. This went on for three days, and by now I was totally fed up being in hospital and just wanted to get home to my own bed.

On the fifth day my wife turned up to visit me in the morning as usual, and I said to her, "I *will* be leaving the hospital before 9 pm tonight." She could see it was still not looking hopeful for me but tried to reassure me that it may be possible. The nurse came along to do her checks that morning, and I said the same thing to her, but she replied that me leaving today would not be happening. That morning I was transferred to another ward and a new nurse was now taking care of me. I said to her that I would be leaving today, but she also repeated what the other nurse had said, and said that I would still be in hospital for a short while longer. By now I was so focused on my command of leaving the hospital by 9 pm that I kept telling my wife and also my daughter when she came to visit. Later in the day my stomach was working, and I was allowed soft solid food like Jell-O. I said to the nurse once more that now I could leave, but she said that tomorrow would still be the earliest I would be allowed to go home.

By 8 pm I was feeling a lot better and our family doctor, who was on her hospital rounds, came to see how I was getting along. She was quite shocked how well I was doing now, and when I asked if I could leave, she said that I had really turned the corner that day and that I could leave if I wanted to, which of course I did want to. I walked out of the hospital at 9 pm that evening, just as I had commanded throughout the day, to the surprise of my family and the nurses.

I learnt a valuable lesson that day: that sometimes you can pick up on intuitive feelings, and sometimes you can send out rockets of desires and ask for manifestations, and *sometimes* you just have to command that something specific happens for the benefit of yourself.

My wife was part of a Mastermind networking group that ran for six months, and they met once every two weeks. At one of the meetings she shared the story of my command in the hospital. At the end of their course all the participants spoke about what they had learned and what had been important to them, and my example of the command was high on their list. I am pleased that her colleagues on her course were able to see the usefulness of the command and will use it in their lives. I hope that you will too.

Imagine And Believe

For anything to happen in life, belief is essential. Everything that you see around you every day, all the cars, computers, televisions, all of it sprang from someone's imagination— imagination tempered with the belief that they were possible—and ended in the definite result. Whatever we want out of our life, however big or small, we need to believe. In The Room there are only positive emotions, so belief is the norm. The world is such a small place nowadays, and there is so much out there for us to explore, achieve and know. Now more than ever before we ought to believe that anything we want out of life is possible.

Alice laughed. "There's no use trying," she said. "One can't believe impossible things. "
"I dare say you haven't had much practice," said the Queen. "When I was your age, I always did it for half an hour a day. Why, sometimes I've believed as many as six impossible things before breakfast. " —Lewis Carroll, *Through The Looking-Glass*

Self-Belief

As well as sometimes lacking belief about what is available to us, we can also possess a lack of self-belief about our own capabilities. We can see things as too hard, too difficult, or even impossible. We may, on occasion, stand back from doing something or involving ourselves in an activity because of a lack of self-belief. A good example for me is dancing. When I used to drink alcohol I would be *brave enough* to dance, but now that I am a teetotaller, I no longer feel comfortable dancing, and have a definite lack of belief in my ability to dance—and I am only talking about dancing at weddings and birthdays, not at a professional dance hall! This is something that I know I need to work on, and it is one of the items on my self-improvement list.

Coming here from our Prior Life experience we believe that anything is possible, but living here in our human existence we can sometimes limit ourselves. When we left The Room we were full of self-belief, if we weren't we would not have made the journey here in the first place. We believed anything was possible and came here to participate and enjoy doing so, knowing that it would be okay. We may all need to find that self-belief inside of us again sometimes in our lives. We need to kick out all doubt, and let in self-belief. We can promote self-belief in our abilities and continue towards our goals and expand our ever growing potential. We can; it is that simple. Let us all believe it and believe in ourselves.

Confidence

Similar to self-belief is confidence. When we have confidence in other people, like family members whom we are close to, we feel safe. When we have confidence in a particular object, like the safety features of a car, we feel safe. When we have confidence in other people, like when someone needs reassurance that they can do a specific job, they feel safe. So, if we can understand these different types of confidence—there are many more—and have confidence in ourselves, we will feel safe. Feeling safe is a positive feeling, one which can form the very foundation of our lives. In Prior Life we all knew that every spirit energy is trustworthy and reliable, and we all knew that coming to Earth and living this human life the way we wanted would happen at the right time. We need to have confidence as much in ourselves as we do in other people.

If we can move from the greatness of self-belief into the power of self-confidence we will have moved further down the road towards fulfilling our potential. This is not to say that you must go parasailing if you do not like heights, but that you must have confidence in your own abilities and participate in the activities that you want to participate in. If you are not afraid of heights and want to learn to parasail, go for it; do not let a lack of self-confidence hold you back, or in this case stop you flying high. Self-confidence comes from within, and we just need to bring it out a bit more sometimes. When we left The Room we were confident that we would end up here living this human existence on Earth—and we did. We were confident that we would continue to grow and learn as we go—and we do. Allow that inner confidence to shine. Be confident in what you do.

Wish Success On Others

With the Law of Attraction you *bring about* what you *think about*. If you are thinking negative thoughts, these will be brought back to you, and if you are thinking positive thoughts, the same is true. Wishing people lots of success and all the best is a natural instinct from our time in The Room, and we can use this knowledge within any aspect of our lives. If you are in business, you can wish your competitors the best. If you are in a sports event you can do the same for the opposition. Promote success and bring success. I would like to offer an example of this—albeit a business example on a small scale. Hopefully it will make it easier to understand and will show the importance of using it in your own life.

We live rurally on Vancouver Island, and for the past six years we have been selling jam from a stand by the side of the road. Although it is not a major industry, we have fun doing it, and it provides us with a little bit of pocket money. This year one of our friends also started making and selling jam and yet another friend is thinking about doing so as well. I could have taken this one of two ways. One way would be to be unhappy about it and loudly mention that this brilliant idea was ours—we have been doing it for six years and in fact some people along our road know us as the jam people—asking that our friends not step on our toes. I could try and dissuade them and talk them into doing something else or say negative things about selling jam and try and put them off. All of these obviously come from a negative emotional perspective and a perception that there will be a lack of income for me. I choose not to go along this road.

Instead I wish my friends all the best. With my friend who is already making jam there are things that she does that I like. I like the way she does her jars, with cloth wrapping on the lids, I know that she is making more flavours than we do, and I like the name that she uses. I also know that there will not be a lack of income for me, as she sells in a different area—I will have my regular customers and she will have hers. I am pleased for her and wish her all the best in her jam making endeavours. In fact, if you are ever in this neck of the woods look out for Mrs. Jones Jam.

I know that this is on a very small scale, but the scale is not important, it is about the feeling and the positive emotions over the negative emotions. When I was running my landscaping businesses, both in the UK and Canada, I did not worry about who spoke about starting a landscaping business and who actually started one, for I knew there was—and always is—enough to go around. The friend who I gave my landscaping business to here has taken it with my best wishes, and I hope he continues to be successful with it. It is not about fearing a lack, but a matter of happily accepting a plentiful supply for all. With genuine wishes of success for others, you are being true to your spirit energy and matching how you are in The Room.

Give credit where credit is due. When anyone has done a good service for you, tell them how pleased you are. Offer to give a company a testimonial for any great work that they may have provided to you. Sometimes in our society, we are quick to tell other people about bad service or bad deals that may be on offer, but not always so quick to talk about good service and deals. Testimonials are a great way to show your gratitude to a particular person or company—they show that you are offering them greater success in the future.

Also be open to reciprocal compliments. What do I mean by that? Well quite simply give compliments to other people on the way they look or what they are wearing and be comfortable receiving any compliments that come your way. Sometimes we are better at complimenting other people than at receiving compliments. You should accept all compliments with the good intentions and positive energy that was meant to accompany them. Wish success on other people, give credit to those who deserve it, and compliment anyone who you feel should receive them. Also remember to accept success, credit, and compliments back when they are given to you.

CHAPTER 8

Why Did I Write This Book Now?

I AM A BIG FAN OF DR. WAYNE DYER AND HAVE READ MANY OF HIS books, and it is with the help of some of his insights that I have been able to overcome my long-standing reservations and finally write this book. In his books he talks about judgments and explains that, when he talks at a seminar, he can have five hundred people attending, all of whom may have differing opinions about what he is saying—so being afraid to do something because of other people's opinions and judgments is not in our best interest. This really resonated with me, and it has allowed me to break my silence and write this book. After all, the big picture is that this book can help people—that some people may judge me for it is small in comparison. Dr. Wayne Dyer also wrote a book called *Excuses Begone,* and after reading that book, I was moved to write this book.

A big reason that I wrote this book is that I am *in the know.* I know what my experience was, and that cannot be taken away from me. Imagine that you meet someone on the street and start talking. Somehow the subject of food comes up.

"I just had a big bowl of cereal for breakfast," you say.

The person you're talking to makes a bit of a face. "No, I don't think that's right. I think you had toast."

What is that person possibly basing *that* on? It makes no sense.

"No," you say, a little perplexed. "It was definitely cereal. I remember quite clearly."

"Sorry," that person says. "I can't accept that. I feel that you had toast, and that's all there is to it."

It's a ridiculous conversation.

The point is that, regardless of what this person *chooses* to believe, you know that you had cereal—you are *in the know*. The second person's wrong belief cannot change the fact that you know what you had for breakfast—after all, it was *your* breakfast.

With me, I am *in the know* when it comes to my Prior Life experience in The Room. I am *in the know* when it comes to my own memories. I have slowly come to terms with the fact that this is what is important because what I know might help many people. I cannot allow some people's beliefs or opinions to stop this book from coming to fruition—its message is meant for a wider audience. I believe that I have a message that will benefit so many people in this world. For instance, when someone loses a loved one, there is a tremendous sadness surrounding the loss. I want this book to help people who have suffered such a loss to understand that there is this truly amazing place called The Room that their loved one has gone to. I want this to be of great benefit to them in their grieving process. I would also like to reiterate to anyone who is afraid of dying, to please understand that death is not the end, and there is this other wonderful realm where a warm, welcome awaits us all. A turning point in my decision to come forward came when I read a book called *The Golden Motorcycle Gang* by Jack Canfield and William Gladstone. This book talks about Jack's experience of coming to Earth, and although his experience does not match mine exactly, there were things in his book that made me think more about my own Prior Life experience. I revisited my memories and thought long and hard about them before deciding to tell my wife the memory that I had been carrying around for my whole life. Her positive response and acceptance encouraged me to share my story for the benefit of others. She believed me and reassured me that others would too, and I would sincerely like to thank her for that.

Because The Timing Is Perfect

When we come from a place of worry or concern—or any negative emotions—this can hinder the natural flow of our lives. When we come from a place of knowing and understanding—positive emotions—our natural flow is unobstructed, and everything happens at the right time and in the right order. When I was in The Room, there was no space–time continuum to contend with, and when I was looking at the Journal in The Room with my teacher, I knew that everything would happen at the perfect time for each experience. That is the same with this book. I've discussed the personal reasons holding me back from writing this book until now, but even beyond that, the timing—in this episode of my life—is right. It is the right time for me, for not only do I feel comfortable writing it and sharing the knowledge from The Room with the world, it is also the right time for other people to read this book, comprehend the information, and understand the insights being offered. I feel that the world population is striving to achieve a more peaceful, accepting, connected and community-minded society. That way of being is exactly as it is in our Prior Lives. The Room holds the key to how it can be replicated here on Earth if we want to create it that way.

I feel that there is a yearning for inner-being and finding out who we really are, and some of the experiences I have written about may help to explain it more. I know what happened through my memory, but science may say that it cannot be proved. Sometimes with science, if it cannot be proved scientifically then it cannot be. I do not care what science may say to my experience, for I do not need science to back me up in any way, shape, or form. When they have developed a machine that can copy my memory and store it on a hard drive for scientific proof I will be happy to oblige, but that will only be proof for the scientific community; I do not need any proof. My proof has been with me my entire life.

The timing is right both for me *and* the world community to write this book now, and the timing is right to learn more about our time as spirit energy in Prior Life. The timing is exactly as my journey and the Journal in The Room predicted it to be.

To Help People Understand

There are some important lessons from The Room that we can all take on board and learn from. We can use these lessons for our own benefit or for the benefit of other people in need of them. As I have already stated, being in The Room is an awesome feeling, and it is a truly great place full of warmth, compassion and acceptance. Having this experience has not always been of benefit to me the way that it should have been. This was due to my own stubborn human resistance, but now I can understand exactly how positive my Prior Life experience is to me, for it has made my life easier to understand in a way that has greatly increased the positivity in my life. I hope that you will be able to transform your life as well. I want people to understand that, regardless of where they are in their life, and however they may be feeling right now, it will be okay.

Coping With Loss

Now I do not want to appear callous, but when I hear that someone has died—or attend a funeral—while my sympathy goes out to the bereaved, I do not mourn for the person who has died, for I know that they are in The Room. It does not mean that I am going to forget them or that I am not upset that they have passed away, but I know that they are happy where they are. My sympathy is aimed towards those family members and friends left behind mourning the loss. This has always been how I have acknowledged the loss of a person—except once.

I have experienced the loss of grandparents, cousins, and friends and have naturally been sad that they have departed—but I've always understood that they have gone back to The Room. The one time it was different was with the loss of our baby, who we lost in the 24th week of pregnancy due to a miscarriage. Despite my knowledge of The Room, I found it very hard to think that he would have not have the human life he came here for, would never get married, would not have children, would not be able to enjoy travelling or any other life-experience that would be open to him. This grief stayed with me for a very long time, including through other deaths where I accepted the loss in my usual way.

It took me a long time to realize that I was really grieving for myself and what I would miss out on; I was grieving for my lost life-experiences with our baby. Deep down I know that he went back to that amazing place called The Room, and he reset his life path and waited for his turn to be born again. Once I fully accepted all of this, I was able to move on again, not forget him but move on. So I know the thoughts and feelings that loved ones have when someone very close and very dear to them passes away, and I know the grieving process that they are going through. I know it can be hard to move on from a loss, but knowing they are in The Room is a very satisfying and heartwarming feeling. I also know how even thinking in this way can be tough, but my hope is that you will be able to see that where the departed have gone is an amazing place—and take solace in that. When you know where they are, I hope you are able to move on in your own time and live again.

We come from The Room, live our human existence, and return to The Room, it is a never-ending cycle.

We Are On A Working Holiday

Our time here on this Earth is but a phase in a cycle. We come from the Room and return to The Room to await our next working holiday here on Earth.

What do I mean by working holiday? Well let me put it this way: When we are born we enter this human existence with eagerness and excitement. We look forward to participating in the human race and giving ourselves over to it entirely. We see ourselves as toddlers, schoolchildren, workers and retirees—there is a certain order to life on Earth. Another way to look at life on Earth is that, at some point, we will all die. The thing is we already existed before we arrived here. As spirit energy we had a special place that we came from and the same special place that we will return to. Our time here on Earth is but a fraction of our entire existence. We are here on a working holiday of sorts, a vacation away from The Room, one which enables us to work on growing our spirit energy, our soul. Our human body may die, but our spirit energy lives on and will continue with its journey. Our spirit energy was alive before this human existence and will live on long after. When we are in The Room, we spend time looking, in a non-judgmental way, at our previous lives and considering the things that we may have done differently, and it is through this process that we determine what we wish to pursue in our next lifetime. We are contemplating a great many things while we are in The Room; that is why I call our life a working holiday. I do not mean that this life we are leading is a chore – in fact it is the complete opposite – it is an adventurous, exciting part of our spirit energies growth. Understanding this can benefit us greatly, for it shows that, even through times of struggle, we can work through our difficulties and grow by way of our trial, for these are the things that we set for ourselves in The Room. This is a healthy, helpful perspective for this working holiday called life.

The Missing Link

There are some great books out there about different stages of life and pre-life. There are great authors who talk about living in the now. There is Anita Moorjani who has written a book, entitled *Dying To Be Me,* about her near death experience. And there are books about past lives by authors such as

Michael Newton who wrote books such as *Destiny of Souls*. All these books discuss many of the diverse stages of life, *except one*—Prior Life and our time in The Room. This is the area the so-called missing link; it completes the chain from past life, to near death, to living in the now.

The information and insights that I have provided in this book are from my own Prior Life experiences in The Room. They give knowledge to us as human beings, which was not necessarily known about before, or if it was at all suggested or referred to it did not have sufficient evidence to back it up. I am now providing that evidence to support any and all of these theories. I am trying to provide as much detail as possible to help us all understand our experiences in Prior Life better and to know that such a wonderful and glorious place as The Room does exist. I am trying to help connect the chain by providing this missing link. Once we put all the links in the chain together, of what we know through other people's experiences, and add my own link to this chain, then the chain is now complete.

The chain runs from Previous Lives, to Prior Life, to the Now Life we are living, sometimes to Near Death, back to The Room and Prior Life once more, to our Next Life and on and on it goes, one continual chain. The Room and Prior Life are the link that completes the chain and can fully enhance our understanding of where we were, where we go, why we go there and, when put with what we already know, gives us a much more complete map of the spirit energy journey. The missing link is missing no more!

CHAPTER 9

A Few Things I Have Learnt In This Human Existence

DURING MY TIME ON EARTH I HAVE LEARNT A LOT ABOUT SOME human traits, some negative and some positive. They affect all of us to one degree or another. The impact of some are a near everyday occurrence, while others are more exceptional. Taken together they make up what it means to be human- ized. As I have mentioned before in this book, the negative traits are uniquely human and earthly while the positive ones also exist in—and probably spring from—The Room.

Anger

This has been quite a big thing for me over the years. Growing up I can remember anger from friends and family members. I can recall some quite angry moments and events involving people in my life, and I know that, for a period of time after witnessing these angry episodes, I got drawn in and nursed my own anger. As a child I mainly only had anger over situations such as stubbing my toe on a door, or when I felt unfairly treated and may miss out on something.

Through my teenage years this grew a bit more inside me, due to my competitive streak in sports and that 'young stag' mentality that adolescent teenage boys may get. During my adult years I have had anger at specific situations; I admit to road rage and shouting and swearing at other drivers; I admit to anger in the work environment, particularly working in the construction field; and I admit to anger in personal times including with my family.

As a child I was smacked whenever I misbehaved—it could be anything from one smack to a few, and given with a hand, a slipper, or anything else that was easy to grab at the time.

From these smacking experiences, the one thing I am very pleased about is that my wife and I set a rule that we would never smack our children, and we never have. No matter how angry I may have been at them for doing something wrong I have always been able to control it with my children. I remember how low, sad, hurt and unloved I felt after being smacked, and I would never want my children—or any child—to feel this way.

In my life today I cannot say I do not have anger, but the occasions where anger may raise its ugly head are less frequent. I seem to think about situations a lot more now before giving in to anger. If I stub my toe on a door, it still hurts, and I can still feel that rage, but now I am more aware that there is no point in the anger because my toe will still ache anyway.

Anger is an ugly trait, and one that is full of negatives. How many people sit in prisons because of anger, after doing something wrong that they would not otherwise have done? With my work in the social care field I have seen some quite angry people and been caught up in a couple of angry situations. Seeing anger firsthand is not nice, neither as a child nor an adult, and it is a very negative energy and emotion to release.

Through working in the counselling environment, particularly working with domestic abuse, I heard about anger nearly every day. Working in that environment can be draining and quite exhausting, but it can also be rewarding, knowing you are helping people escape anger and move on from abusive relationships. When I did that job, I can remember thinking that I did not know that there was this much anger around in our society, and it was quite a sad feeling.

All of us may have anger about some things, but it is how we deal with it that is important. If we feed our anger it will grow and can escalate the problem, but if we can understand it and work with it, the problem can soon diminish. I am comfortable enough to hold my hand up and say that anger has been aimed at me and by me. Anger has been thrust towards me from others, and I have pushed my anger towards others. In either situation, as the receiver or giver of anger, deep down I have not felt comfortable with the way I was feeling, and I know I do not want those feelings again. I have also felt anger at myself for allowing the anger to surface in the first place. When anger strikes, try and conquer it. Think about the situation and why it has arisen, determine if anger is even warranted at all, decide how else the situation could be handled without anger and allow the anger to subside. When you have done this a few times, it can just become routine. I know that I do not want anger in my life, for my life is better without it. If we can all banish or control our anger the world would benefit greatly.

I think that sometimes negative emotions, like anger, can confuse us, for they are human emotions not spirit energy emotions. When we are in The Room there is no anger—only love—so when anger presents itself in our human life, we do not always know what to do with it. Subsequently we sometimes feed our anger, which can lead to regret later on at the outcome. Learning how to live with and deal with anger is a great step forward to positive living—living in the way that is natural for us as spirit energy.

Denial

Denial can be something that is frustrating for us to see if we are unable to overcome it. For me an easy example of this would be witnessing denial in my alcohol counselling work. I saw many different people over the years I worked as an alcohol counsellor, and each person was at a different stage of their drinking—from not being sure if they even had an alcohol issue, to fully understanding that they were drinking too much and needing help.

I worked with people who wanted different outcomes from the counselling. Some people wanted abstinence from alcohol—to stop drinking altogether. Some people wanted to *control* their drinking—not fully stop—but be able to drink while being in control of the amount that they drink. Sometimes these people wanted to be able to drink at special occasions like weddings or birthdays.

With other people we looked at the issue in terms of harm reduction; in these cases they tended to be heavier drinkers who may not really want to stop drinking—perhaps they wanted to cut back from ten beers a day to five. I would do whatever I could to help them achieve their goals. I also worked with the significant others—the partners of people with alcohol issues—and with this group the drinking partner did not need to be clients of the agency for us to see the significant other. I would sometimes see people who would walk into the counselling room, tell me exactly what their problem was and articulate the end result they wished to achieve. They would be focused, primed for success, and ready for the road ahead. Working with them in the twelve sessions would be a breeze, and watching them leave at the end of their twelve sessions, having achieved what it was they set out to achieve, was very heartwarming.

When I worked with the harm-reduction group they may already have said that they do not want to stop—just cut down for the benefit of their health, their wallet, their family or all three. With this group, some would succeed in their goal where others would not. If they were able to cut down on their alcohol consumption, then it was a great result for them, but if the result was not reached they were always welcomed back to try again when they were ready.

Then there were those in denial…

The denial took many forms: denial of how much alcohol they really drank, denial of their true goals, even denying that a problem existed at all. Sometimes when I asked someone how much they were drinking they'd say, "A bottle of wine a day, and that's a problem for me" –or– "A bottle of wine a day at this point, and I want to draw the line there. "When I asked someone who was in denial the answer would be, "Y'know I don't even know why I'm here, I only drink a couple of beers on the weekend" –or– "My drinking's fine, I can stop whenever I want" –or– "I only drink one or two beers a day. Well more like three or four, with more on Friday and Saturday nights, but otherwise it's five or six a day. "

With each of these scenarios is a denial factor. With the first scenario I would already know a rough amount of the alcohol they consumed from the person who referred them, perhaps their family doctor. With the second scenario this could easily be discounted by asking if they had stopped drinking before, and if the answer was something along the lines of, "I did for a couple of days a short while back, but I soon started again, and I have tried since and managed a day here and there," then this showed that they struggle to stop drinking on their own and will need the support on offer to them. With the third scenario, I have heard this on a number of occasions, where the amount of alcohol being consumed slowly rises throughout the counselling session and has actually doubled, if not more, by the end of the session. Once clients I counselled worked through their denial—or released it altogether—I saw some quite big improvements in their focus. With denial they may have been coming for counselling for six weeks without any changes to their drinking, but once they break the denial bond they really take the bull by the horns and significantly move towards their target goal. The denial was part of what was been holding them back and being able to make the shift away from denial was an important step for them. Once the denial has been recognized and dealt with, it is amazing what results can come to fruition.

I am using these scenarios not to show weaknesses in certain people or to upset people who may be reading this thinking, *geez, that's me.* I am using them to illustrate how denial can be at work within us. It is something that we may all have used at some stage of our life—and may still be using today.

Denial can occur for a number of reasons. It can be due to shame and embarrassment; people may think that if they admit their problem to themselves that they will have have let themselves or others down. It can be due to being in trouble with others; as children if we were always punished when we admitted something then we may learn to survive punishment by using denial. It can also be due to genuinely not knowing what it is you are doing; an example of this is with a drinker suddenly counting up and realizing that they drink three bottles of wine a day, not the one to two bottles they thought they drank.

As I said, denial can be for a number of reasons, and it's certainly not exclusive to people with alcohol issues—those were just examples to illustrate denial. I have fallen prey to denial myself in the past. I have had denial about being overweight and the amount of food I was eating. I have had denial when it comes to my level of fitness, wanting to believe that I was still as fit as I used to be when I played soccer. I have had denial about what I am capable of. I have had denial about my Prior Life memories and my time in The Room and kept them hidden inside of me. These are all denials, but I have slowly overcome them. I had to face facts that I was eating too much, and since doing so, I have lost weight and improved my quality of life. I have accepted that through not exercising I cannot be as fit as I used to be, and I have started doing fitness programs with my wife and feel a lot better for it. For many years I thought that I would never get a higher level of education, but I achieved my counselling diploma, and now know that if I set my mind on something, then it is possible. I hid my Prior Life memory for over forty years. Now I am putting it into words in this book in hopes of benefitting those who read it.

Denial does not have to be a part of our lives, and we just need to recognize this. I am not denying that there are probably more things in my subconscious that I am denying, but when they come to the fore, I hope to be able to work through them. There is a funny saying: *Denial ain't just a river in Egypt.* It'd be a better world if it was; deny the denial.

Realization

Moving on from denial is realization. Realization is the opposite of denial. It is the perception or comprehension of the potential in ourselves and other people. Realization can be a quick, *lightbulb* moment or slowly dawning over a period of time. It can be rewarding to know what it is you have realized, for it exemplifies growth in your life.

I have had realization a few times in my life. I realized, at a quite early age, that I could play soccer quite well. I realized that fun and laughter is a huge requirement in my life. I realized that my family is very important and special to me. I realized that the world has changed from a large place to a small place, and that travelling and exploring is relatively easy and accessible nowadays compared to when I was younger. I have realized what has meaning to me and what does not. I have realized that I want to fill my life with the positives and reject the negatives. I have realized the importance of love, not just just sharing it with the obvious people in our lives, but the importance of love for all. I have realized the importance of forgiveness in releasing baggage and moving on with our lives without that negative stigma attached. I have realized the wondrous beauty of Mother Nature. I have realized many things and will continue to do so.

And we have all realized our human lives here on Earth today, otherwise we would never have left The Room to live, experience, and enjoy them.

Responsibility

Responsibility is one of those words that can be nice if we are being described as responsible, and can be scary if we are being asked to be responsible for something. I can think of times in my life where I have been responsible and been proud of it, times I've been given responsibility and carried it through precisely. I can also think of times in my life when I have been irresponsible and not so proud and been given responsibility and not lived up to it. Responsibility, or a lack thereof, can also bring out denial. If we break something we can either take responsibility and say that we broke it or retreat into denial and say that we do not know how it broke.

We all have different responsibilities in life. Some responsibilities are for ourselves and some responsibilities are for other people. For ourselves we are responsible for many things including our behaviour, our debts, our health and the upkeep of our homes. For others, we may have responsibilities for our children, our pets, our co-workers, our teammates. Within society we strive to be responsible citizens.

Responsibility need not be a burden and should not be an excuse to bring denial into the equation. I have not always stood up to responsibility and have denied losing, breaking or damaging something. I have not always been responsible in my behaviour or with my health. The good thing about responsibility is that you can become responsible at any time. I now take responsibility for things I break. I take responsibility for my actions, whether good or bad. If they are good I can promote them to use another time, if they are bad, I can look at them and learn from them. Responsibility comes with the territory of life, and we should not be afraid of responsibility or run and hide from it.

Gratitude

Gratitude, thanks and appreciation are three powerful words that we can all use with aplomb. Being grateful is a positive state of mind that enhances our thoughts and feelings about something in particular. A thank you is free, yet very rewarding to both the thanked and the thanker. There are many things that we should be grateful for and many things over the course of our lives for which we should show appreciation. I am happy to share some of mine with you—I say *some,* for this really is the tip of the iceberg when it comes to things for which I am grateful.

I am grateful for allowing my spirit energy the opportunity to come and live this life as a human being. I am grateful for the contrasts that have been in my life; without these I would not have been able learn what I've learnt. I am grateful for my wife, my children and all the family members I have now, all I have known in the past, and all I will know in my future. I am grateful for all the friends I have had in the past, all the friends I have in my present, and all the friends I will have in my future. I am grateful for the wonderful pets I have in my life today and all the wonderful pets that I have been lucky enough to have before. I am thankful for the magnificent nature that surrounds us every day. I am grateful for the house we call home and for all the other homes that have given me shelter in my time here on Earth. I am grateful for the possessions that I have had that have made my life comfortable. I am grateful for the food and water that has sustained my life. I am grateful for having love in my life, both giving and receiving love. I am grateful for all the countries and places I have visited and for all those I have still to visit. I am grateful for all the experiences and memories with which my life has presented me. I am grateful for my Prior

Life memories from in The Room and having the ability to share these wondrous insights to the world. I am grateful for many things. I am grateful.

Actualization

When you think of doing a certain something and put a plan in place to do that, and you end up with the result of having the opportunity to experience that something, that can be called actualization. When you think of something, allow it to happen, and that something then presents itself and materializes, that can be called actualizing. When you are being as you really are, that can be called you being actual.

Actualization is a great mode of bringing experiences in to enhance our life. It can be one of many things including travelling to a country of your choice, seeing a Wonder of the World, enjoying a trip or vacation that you have always dreamed about, or living in a different country other than your birth country and participating in new cultural activities.

Actualizing can be of major benefit in bringing things forth in your life. That car you have always wanted and have now saved up enough for and bought. That house you always wanted to live in and now own and call home. That pet that you always wanted and now share a special bond with.

Being actual is the way you can live your life. When we are being actual in our lives, we are displaying who we are, with the essence coming from a genuine and congruent way.

When we were in The Room we were actual—nothing hidden; we put it all on the line. We were actualizing the events that we wanted in this life, and we actualized our human life by coming to Earth to live it. As humans we can carry on these skills and actually have a very actualizing experience.

Give Others A Chance

How many times have we looked at people and judged them on how they look, and how many times have we decided that something is not for us without even trying it. I know I have refused food saying I did not like it, whereas in reality I have never tried it before; I just did not like the look of it. I know I have not gone to an event because my thought pattern was that it would be boring or not something that I would enjoy, but I had never participated in anything like it before, so how would I know?

I would like to share an example of something that happened to me recently that reinforces this. I really enjoyed watching the London Olympics, and whenever I was able I would watch as much of it as I could. There were sports that I already liked and watched and others that I thought I would probably like, so I viewed those as well and found them fun to watch. On the last day of the Olympics I was flicking through the television channels after watching the men's basketball final and the only other Olympic sport that I could see being shown was rhythmic gymnastics. Now I have never watched rhythmic gymnastics before, but I instantly sighed in disappointment and continued flicking through the channels until I realized I would have to watch that or nothing. With great trepidation, I flicked back to the rhythmic gymnastics and watched from a point of view that at least watching this was better than nothing. In less than a minute, I was hooked. It was a team event, and all the members of the team had balls that they were throwing up, down, to the side, everywhere really, and the other team members would catch them without looking and roll them to another teammate, all the time while doing gymnastics. Believe me, these girls had better ball control than some NBA players! I was transfixed at what I was watching and was really quite upset when we had to go out and I was unable to watch any more. I will definitely be looking out for this in the next Olympics and watching it with glee.

This was another kick in the pants to me and another of those life lessons that we quite often find ourselves learning. Sometimes we are too quick to dismiss someone or something without giving them a chance. Sometimes we can make up our minds about an individual without them even having a chance to show us who they really are. When we are in The Room we all have the same opportunities, the same chance, regardless what level of our journey we are on. As you can see from the example I used, giving someone or something a chance can be beneficial to yourself as well as them. I would never have known that I would have enjoyed rhythmic gymnastics so much if I had not given it a chance. Give other people a chance and chance the other people.

Give Yourself A Chance

The flip side to giving other people a chance is giving yourself a chance. Giving other people a chance and giving yourself a chance are both great skills that enable us all to move on with life in a natural flow. As human beings we can be quite quick to punish or beat ourselves up over something that we may have done wrong or said out of turn or not fully understood. We need to realize that, on occasion, we will all *put our foot in it,* but we mustn't be too hard on ourselves; we must be able to move on. If I were to beat myself up after every time that I may have made a mistake or misread a situation, I would have spent the last thirty-five years laying in a hospital bed bandaged from head to toe! Sometimes we need to realize that it is okay and not as bad as first feared—that everything will be all right in the end. We can all make mistakes in our lives, but we can all move on from them as well. If we are really being intense with our emotions, over some perceived fault, then we must forgive ourselves, releasing the tension and allowing ourselves back into the flow again.

We also need to be more aware of what we are capable of within ourselves. If we want to participate in a certain activity, but are unsure about what others may think—or unsure if it is even possible—then we need to block out any negative talk, whether from others or ourselves, and try it. I am not saying that we should all become cliff divers in Hawaii, but if it is something which we feel is possible for us, and we have the desire, why not do it? I know for myself that I absolutely love speed, but am not great with heights. I have had the opportunity to race around Brands Hatch race track in the UK twice and thoroughly enjoyed it. I would do it again in a heartbeat. I have also had the opportunity to go up in a hot air balloon in the UK and go zip-lining here in Canada. I know my limitations, but I also know what I want to try and what I would feel comfortable doing; I had a tremendous time on the hot air balloon trip and would not hesitate to do it again. I passed on the zip-lining but enjoyed listening to the stories of those who went and enjoyed seeing their photos. Even though the ballooning involve heights I felt okay giving it a try, and I was happy that I did. I was also okay turning zip-lining down—I am happy *that* I did that as well. Give yourself a chance to enjoy what you may be comfortable doing.

Lost And Found

Sometimes life can be a bit like the lost and found department in a busy train station. You can lose yourself in a downward spiral or find yourself floating along on cloud nine. We can all lose and find ourselves at some stage of our lives. We can lose our drive and focus on different desires and ambitions, yet find these again or move into new wants and goals.

If you find yourself a little lost, just stop and take stock and think about what it would take to find yourself again. Use your mind to visualize the *you* that you want to be. Similarly if you are losing interest in a particular hobby, seek out your new passion and involve yourself heartily once more. Being lost does not mean you have to stay lost, and being found can enable your stability and growth. Just because you have a particular interest in a certain activity, if you lose the desire for doing it, do not be afraid to allow yourself to either rekindle your desire for it once more, or move on to another interest that is beckoning you forward.

Watch out and support any family members and friends that may be looking a little lost, and help them in any way that you can—help them find themselves. Being lost is not forever, being found can be.

Be Open-Minded

Being open-minded means being receptive to new ideas, opinions, and possibilities. As human beings we have been socialized in a certain way, with a system of beliefs that purports to tell us right from wrong. This can be both good and bad, and the two need to be separated. Having laws in place that tell us right and wrong and keep the world a safe place and as crime free as possible is a good thing. It is nice to feel safe as citizens living in our particular societies.

But societal belief systems are not perfect, and they tend to err on the side of close-mindedness. As a child growing up in the seventies there was a lot of prejudice against homosexuals. In those days, and indeed through later years, being homosexual was not highly accepted, and a lot of homosexuals hid their relationships. Times have changed. We have come a long way since the seventies and our minds are now more open. Today it is not unusual to see a homosexual couple or hear someone talk about a homosexual friend. This is a huge step in the right direction; it removes the stigma that homosexuals may feel, and allows them to not have to hide like once they did. Kudos to a large part of society for learning, being open-minded and accepting. But this is only the beginning—there is still a sizable percentage of the population that does not accept this, and we need to assist in their becoming open-minded. I am using the homosexual example to get a point across, but there are any number of groups being discriminated against.

When we are in The Room, there is no discrimination, only acceptance; no hate, only love; and no outcasts, only togetherness. With each other's help, we can teach ourselves to open up our minds to the differences around us, by reminding ourselves we are all Differently The Same. Once that fundamental message is reinforced and embraced by society, we can live happy, peaceful lives, free of discrimination.

Move From Am I? To I Am!

I know that there are many instances in my life where I have been a unsure of myself: unsure of being able to do a particular activity, unsure of doing a particular job, unsure what to say at a certain event. I also know that I may have questioned some things by asking—*am I...?*

Am I smart enough?

Am I capable?

Am I qualified?

These questions shows that we may hope we are, but we are not one hundred percent sure. When we ask *am I...*, it shows that we are not confident with the answer. When I played soccer and played in my regular defensive position, I could say, without a doubt, *"I am a defender."* If I had to play midfield, I knew that I had to say, *"I am a midfielder."* in order to play that position comfortably and to full effect. I could not play to my potential asking, *"Am I a midfielder?"*

I know that I have areas in my life that I will have to change from *am I* to *I am.* I know that for me to write this book I changed my thoughts to *I am an author,* from *am I an author?* Regardless of whether I write any more books or not, the fact that I have written this one means I can say, *"I am an author."* When we are in The Room we *are*—that's it. We know we are, we are glad we are, and we are very comfortable knowing that we are. I will work on moving more of my thoughts away from *am I* and into *I am.* I know it will benefit my life and what I believe myself capable of in the future.

CHAPTER 10

The Importance Of It All

THE IMPORTANCE OF IT ALL IS SOMETIMES LOST IN TRANSLATION. What is clear in The Room can be obscured on Earth. It can be lost when talking to or about other people. It can be hidden from us by a mountain of different reasons. It can be hidden from us by ourselves, *deliberately*.

What Is Important?

There are big things that are important and there are small things that are important. There are individual things that are important and collective things that are important. There are specific things that may be important to some people and specific things that may be important to other people. What is important to me might not be important to you or vice versa. What is important can be subjective. That being said, there are things that are objectively important to all of us, and they always have been and always will be. It is just that we may have forgotten the importance of it all.

When I look up soccer scores, it is important to me that my team win. Is this important to you? Probably not. When you are parachuting from a plane at four thousand feet, you want to make sure you have a parachute. Is this important to you? Most definitely. We are at a sports event with sixty thousand screaming fans and we do not even make eye contact as we are at opposite ends of the stadium, is this important to you? Again, probably not. If we are in an elevator together and it is stuck between floors, and we both appreciate that we need to get help to get the elevator free and work together to escape, is this important to you? Yes, absolutely.

Sometimes individual things may or may not be important to one or more people. Sometimes group things may be important to one or more people. Sometimes group things are important to everyone in that group. What is important is what is important to me, you and other people.

What Is Important To Us All?

Throughout this book I have touched on different areas of our lives and different emotions, thoughts and feelings that are important to us, both individually and as a whole. I would like to talk about some of them a bit more here and bunch some of them together to show the amount of importance these things can have. They are all important to us all.

The Importance Of My Prior Life Experience In The Room

Everything that I have written about is from the memory that I have carried around with me my whole life, from my Prior Life experience in The Room. The messages, insights and knowledge that I have spoken about is intended to give everyone a clearer understanding of exactly what it is like there, and how it can also be here in our human lives, with a little effort from ourselves. The vision that I am portraying of The Room is precisely how I remember it, and I have only written about what I can remember, as I refuse to guess how it should or should not be for any information that I cannot recall at this time. If and when further memories are *released from storage* I will talk about those at that time. The memories I have now are what is important for this time, as they already provide plenty of information for how we can all be more accepting and understanding, and be on track for making our lives in our human existence better for everybody, including ourselves.

The Importance Of Becoming Humanized And Human Feelings

These two fit together very nicely because the first one talks about what we go through when we come to these human lives and the other talks about some human feelings that we learn only as human beings, as these emotions and thoughts do not exist in The Room. Becoming humanized is really the path we all take to live and grow in our societies, and if studies were done around the world at various locations, there would be different humanizations taking place depending on the need for each different society. What we can learn from this is that, when we become humanized, we do have a choice of what human feelings we take on with us. I knew this more than anybody, yet I still let outside voices influence me, and I freely admit that it was not for the better. Now I am free to make my own choices about what human feelings I wish to take on and which ones I can leave behind. This is the same for you as well. Only take the human feelings that you wish to have. Becoming humanized just became a little easier.

The Importance Of Valuable Lessons From The Room

With this one I am going to talk about each lesson individually—as they are all important elements and lessons—and then I will talk about them all together and show the importance of them all being valuable lessons as a whole.

Love is the essence of life both here on Earth and in The Room. There is a song called "Love Is A Many-Splendored Thing" that has been sung by a few different singers and the song title is very true. Love is one of the most important elements of our biological make-up, as both spirit energy and human beings. With love anything is possible; we can all live together in harmony and—as we may all have been told at some time in our lives—love conquers all.

Important qualities are, as the name suggests, important and we should realise and accept that. Show the world your important qualities and be proud of them.

We all need to recognize when Ego is showing itself too much and too often in our lives, and we need to realize when we have to step in and deny ego. We can do this whenever we want, so please do not allow ego to tell you that it is not possible.

Sometimes we may need to take stock of the situation and Look Inside And See Ourselves, for more clarity of how we are doing in this human existence and the journey we are on. Looking inside and seeing yourself will enable you to know what it is that you want, how you are feeling about it, and accept that you will be able to get it.

When you Look Inside And See The Other Person, you look through the human body that is presented before you and into the *real* person that may be hidden inside. Looking inside and seeing the other person enables you to give them a chance and help them to free the *real* them and be the person who they really are.

Empathy is one of the strongest and most powerful words that I have written in this book. With empathy we respond to peoples situations with the understanding that we have in The Room, and we are able to expand our spirit energy emotions into our human being existence. When this is done by more and more people, the positive enhancement to our everyday world will be huge and of significant benefit to everyone.

Being A Rescuer is a skill that we can do both on purpose and without knowing that we are doing it. When we are being a rescuer, we are showing that we care for somebody and that we will help them in their moment of need. We can all learn when being a rescuer is appropriate in our lives.

Having Fun And Excitement is another one of those musts in life that we sometimes put on the back burner. Having fun and excitement can help release stress and tensions from our lives and, as we may have been told before, laughter is the best medicine.

Forgiveness can be one of the hardest emotions for us to carry through with, but when we forgive, we can enhance our lives so much—by releasing extra, worthless baggage— that in time we can look back and wonder why we did not forgive before.

When we forgive we Release emotions, but we also need to realize that we can release emotions at any time. We can release negative emotions from our being and allow more of the positive emotions to replace them.

Staying in Alignment is important for us if we are to stay on the right track—where we set out from and where we intend to go to on our life journey. If we can stay in alignment, we can have more focus towards the goal ahead of us.

When we Trust The Process, we send out a very powerful message that we trust—rather than doubt—the route of our journey. Trusting the process means that we are allowing things to come into our lives that will benefit us and other people and that we believe in what we have chosen for ourselves on this journey.

Sharing love, having important qualities, denying ego, looking inside and seeing yourself, looking inside and seeing the other person, showing empathy, being a rescuer, enjoying fun and excitement, allowing forgiveness, accepting releases, staying in alignment and trusting the process—these are all valuable lessons from The Room, both individually and taken as a group. Each one is either glowing in its own right or is pushing down negatives and shining the light on positivity. When we are in The Room, the positive features are there with us and are all part of our natural spirit energy. When we come to these human lives we can—and often do unfortunately—pick up some negative features as well. Using these valuable lessons individually or together, we are able to work through issues and deny any negatives so that we can move on with our journey. Each valuable lesson listed here is an important tool in the combined toolbox. Lessons are for learning, so learn these valuable lessons and move on to the next one and teach them to other people so that they can use them too.

The Importance Of We Are
All Differently The Same

I am putting all the sub-headers under this one umbrella again because, being the title of the book, this is a very important message for all of us indeed. When we are having our Prior Life experience in The Room, we are all the same. We may be on different levels of our journey, but there is no competition or battles for position in The Room, so we really are all the same. When we come to live these human lives, we are born in our human bodies. Some of the characteristics will be the same—for example we are all flesh and blood—but there are characteristics that may be different: these can include languages and skin colour. There may also be different cultures and traditions that are observed, and we may witness people with a different sexual orientation or who practice other religions. What we may observe, as human beings, are the differences. What we may not understand, as human beings, is the sameness.

You see, wherever you may be on this Earth, at any particular moment in time, regardless of ethnicity, sexuality, religious belief or any other difference that may be viewed from a human perspective, we are all Differently The Same. It does not matter what the person looks like or what their particular preferences may be or how they act; we are all Differently The Same. When we are in The Room, as spirit energy, we are all the same. When we are living as human beings we are all Differently The Same. Look past any differences, and see the sameness. Once we can all do that, as a worldwide community, we can improve the lives of many people. It is very important that we realize and understand that we are all Differently The Same.

The Importance Of Living
As A Whole Person

In life we can instantly be put into two defining groups and these groups are male and female. In society there may be certain roles that are seen as gender specific and encouraged. Doing something that is not in your gender role can be discouraged. Yet why is that? As a person we have a gender, be it male or female, but if a male wants to participate in a particular activity that is seen as a female role and is good at doing it, why should they be discouraged? And vice versa. When we are having our Prior Life Experience in The Room there are no male or female roles, just a oneness, a completeness. With equality and greater opportunities in the world today, we can break down some of these male and female roles and open them up to either gender. We can break the mould and allow everyone to participate in whichever roles they wish to in their lives.

The Importance Of Intuitiveness

When we are intuitive, we are being focused and in the know. How often do we hear someone say—or even say ourselves—that we knew something would happen because we felt it intuitively. When we are in The Room, we communicate intuitively and know exactly what is going on around us. Bringing that into our human existence can be a definite bonus for us to do. Using intuition is something that some people may find easy and some not so easy, but if we can get that intuitiveness back inside of us we can enjoy what it can offer.

When we use intuition with nature, this is quite a special thing. We may already do it with our pets to a degree, and if we can advance that to wild animals and insects, think how much greater our sense of connection to the natural world. I know that, in my own life, I have felt intuitive with some pets, wild animals and insects. I know how important it is for both me and them to feel safe and to understand their purpose in the world. Finding our intuition within ourselves and with each other and nature is another step forward and should not be dismissed too lightly. For example, when we have a intuitive understanding with wild animals around us, we can better live together. Recognize the importance of intuitiveness, and allow it into your own life.

The Importance Of The Law Of Attraction

One of the best lessons that I have learnt in this life is the Law of Attraction. Looking back, I realize that I was subject to it before understanding it. The Law of Attraction is an important part of my life and can be an important part of your life too.

Realize that negative thoughts attract more negativity and positive thoughts attract more positivity. With this in mind choosing what thoughts you are sending out is a pretty easy decision.

When we want to manifest something into our lives we send out our Rockets Of Desire into the Universe, and these are then manifested to us. It can be that easy, but is not always, as we do not always Allow things to manifest as they otherwise would. We can have doubts that they will materialize or we can just get impatient. It is important we use the Law of Attraction in the right way if we are to manifest our desires.

Sometimes we need to be more forceful and use the Command—this can bring forward a thought or action that we have released into the Universe. I have used this to my benefit when I wanted to leave hospital after having a ruptured appendix and will use it in future situations when the time is right.

To help us manifest our desires through the Law of Attraction, we must imagine and believe that it is coming to us. We need to kick out all doubt and be open and willing and ready to accept whatever it is we asked for. We need to be confident that it will show up in our lives and be grateful when it does.

The Law of Attraction can seem harder than it needs to be, but once you understand it more, and realize how the Law of Attraction works, it can be very beneficial to you and other people around you. You will begin to appreciate what a great life tool we all have surrounding us all the time. The Law of Attraction has a definite place in my life.

The Importance Of Why Did I Write This Book Now?

When is the correct time to write a book? When was the correct time to write this book? Should I have written it when I was still a child? What about writing it when I was a teenager or early adult? Perhaps I should have written it ten years ago? But I did not write it at any of these times in my life. So why is it the right time to write this book now?

Sometimes in life there are situations when you know it is perfect time to do something. In my life, my wife and I agreed on the perfect time to get married. We agreed on the perfect time to have our son and daughter. We agreed on the perfect time to immigrate to Canada. I knew when it was the perfect time to change careers. I knew when it was the perfect time to return to college and get my counselling diploma. And there are more times when I knew the timing was perfect. It was the same when it came writing this book; the perfect time was now.

For me there was one important obstacle to writing this book; I did not feel comfortable telling anyone about my memory. If I could not tell anyone about my memory, how could I possibly write a book about it? Now that I have told a few people the details about my memory, I have found writing this book to be very easy, and I have enjoyed writing it and sharing my memory and insights from the Room. I know that I have made a shift, and I believe that the world is making a shift as a whole. I hope that people will find this book helpful to them. This is why it was important that I write this book now.

The Importance Of Coping With Loss

As human beings we will all suffer the loss of a loved one at some point in our lives. How we cope with that may vary depending on the individual concerned. I wrote this book to share an understanding that, as spirit energy, we have a Prior Life experience in The Room. During this time we are born and live our lives as human beings. At the end of these human lives our bodies die but our spirit energy returns to The Room. I feel that it is important to share this knowledge with those who have lost a loved one so that they can understand where they have gone. It is important, too, for those who may be afraid of dying so that they know it will be okay. It is just our human body that dies, our spirit energy lives on. We will all, at some stage in the future, leave our human bodies and return to that amazing place I call The Room.

I know that, when I suffered a particularly close loss, I was lost for a while. I know that I was looking to blame and be angry at something or someone. I know that I worked through some stages of the grief process but got stuck in others. When I accepted what had happened—that our baby had returned to The Room—I was able to move on. Remember, I have already had this knowledge for my whole life, yet I still did not want to accept it. I hope that what I have written about will allow you to work through the grieving process a little easier.

The Importance Of We Are On A Working Holiday And The Missing Link

As humans we can sometimes look at things as having a timespan. When we buy a television, we expect to have it for a period of time before we need to replace it. When we buy a car, we expect it to run for so long before we need to change it for another car. This is the same with our lives. We may think that we come here, live for a number of years and then die; the end. In fact we were alive *before* we came here. We had our Prior Life experience in The Room, and after our human bodies die we will return to The Room. Our time here on earth is our working holiday. We are here for our spirit energy to learn valuable lessons to enable it to move along on its chosen journey.

The information that I am providing in this book fits perfectly into a chain consisting of experiences of past lives, living in the now and near death. The experience of being in The Room is the missing link that completes the chain and makes it whole. Realizing that the information I have written gives details about how we are on earth on a working holiday, and also provides details on it being the missing link, is important. When we can understand both of these components, we can free ourselves to enjoy our working holidays more, knowing that, with the understandings of the missing link—our Prior Life experiences—we will all return to The Room one day.

The Importance Of A Few Things I Have Learnt In This Human Existence

When I look at this chapter, I look at the important issues that have been in my life and how I have dealt with them. I can see some things that may seem obvious but which, obvious or not, we are not always good at doing—and I can hold my hands up to that as well. Some things seem to be so comprehensible that they do not *appear* to require effort on our part, but we can subsequently end up not doing them through lack of effort. Some of these things I have worked on and now do on a regular basis. Some I am still working on and will improve with over time.

The Importance Of Realization, Denial And Responsibility

If we stay in denial, we are unable to reach realization and unable to take responsibility for our lives. In some circumstances we may deliberately attempt to stay in denial as a way to avoid acting responsibly. When we are facing difficult things in life, denial can feel like a safe place, a haven from problems that may be trailing us. If we stay in denial, we do not have to deal with them. Unfortunately, if we stay in denial we are also unable to move on clearly with our particular journey in life. When we are in denial, we may start by not always seeing a way out, but when we start making realizations we may see the way through. Now comes the tricky part. If we can see the way through with realization, we know we can move on through it, but to do that would mean leaving our comfort blanket of denial and taking on a new mantra of responsibility. This does not need to be scary.

We came here from The Room as responsible spirit energy with a realization of what a human life could be. We took on any denial that we have when we were humanized, and we can shed that skin and move back into our true selves just as easily. Exploring the realization of what we are capable of, and being responsible for our thoughts, emotions and actions stand us in better stead for our authentic self. Deny denial any victories and realize responsibly exactly where you are heading and what you can accomplish along the way.

The Importance Of Gratitude And Actualization

There are many things in life that we may want and wish for. Some of these may present themselves to you at some stage of your life. When they do they are actualizing themselves to you. When you receive something that you have asked for be grateful for receiving it and in this way more actualizations may come to you that you may have asked for. Being grateful is high up on the list of emotions that we should be manufacturing inside of ourselves. I have had people tell me about how bad their day has been and listened to them reel of a list of bad things. I have asked what good things have happened to them that day and they have an equally long list, but are just focusing on the negatives of the day and not being grateful for the positives. Having gratitude is a positive emotion and if we promote gratitude to the things that turn up in our lives we are promoting more positive actualizations. Being grateful is an important quality to possess.

The Importance Of The Importance Of It All!

When I wrote this chapter, I wanted to make it a little bit like a refresher of the main course. In other words, I wanted to open up some more of what I have already written in the other chapters and to show this learning in a condensed form. I also wanted to show how some of the sub-headers can work together in groups as well as individually. Because of my Prior Life experience in The Room, I feel that every single word I have written in this book is important, and I really want to clarify how everything in this book all ties together for the greater good of humankind, from all the insights and lessons from The Room. Each one has an importance, individually, that we can take on and learn from, and each one has an importance together with others that we can also gain knowledge about. I really cannot emphasize enough the importance of my Prior Life experience and what I have learnt from it. Even though I have kept it hidden inside me until this year, I can now see the importance of passing this message out to the world to share.

The Importance Of In Conclusion

The importance of this chapter is that it enables me to talk about what I see for my future and what the future may hold for others. I can talk about what I am leaving behind and the direction I see myself heading. It also gives me a chance to talk about a few different sub-headers that were not put under specific chapters in this book but still have important messages within them nonetheless. I will not talk about the chapter too much, as it is the next one and you have not read it yet, but I am pleased to be able to cover a few more topics and enlarge further the experiences I had in my Prior Life.

Why These Are Important

I cannot reiterate enough how important these segments are. I remember that, when I was at school, I would be given lines to do if I did something wrong. The lines were repetitive and taught me that what I was writing about: "I must not shout in the classroom," for example, was copied lots of times to imprint the message into me. That is the way I have written this book. I really want to imprint the importance of Prior Life, The Room, the knowledge, the insights and the understanding of these things so that it can benefit both our own lives and the lives of those around us. Sometimes just talking about something once is not enough, and details are lost. I hope that, by talking about them individually in their specific chapters, they gave you the information required to understand the qualities of each one, and I hope that putting them as sub-headers together here shows how all these things work together in the bigger scheme of things. We can never stop learning enough, and we can never underestimate the importance of it all. Please understand the importance of this.

CHAPTER 11
In Conclusion

I HAVE NO REGRETS IN THE WAY MY LIFE HAS GONE. I HAVE HAD great times. I have had sad times. I have loved and been loved. Everything that has happened to me has happened for a reason. Everything that happens to me in the future will continue to happen to me for a reason. I recognize that these are parts of the formation of our lives.

My Future

From reading books from authors like Esther and Jerry Hicks, Dr. Wayne Dyer and others, I am really comfortable living my life with a definite emphasis on the positive aspects of things. I aim to continue experiencing fun and laughter and to allow the excitement of life to shine through. Remembering back to when I was a child living with my in-The-Room memories and my Prior Life experience, I was a lot more positive naturally. I was definitely a lot more excited about things, even the simple things in life. I would like to rekindle that as best I can and have many more exciting times. I would like to continue with the experiences I enjoy having now and expand my experiences continually.

I will work on recovering more memories from The Room and my Prior Life experience. I am aiming to increase both my intuitive awareness in my life and the silent communication with nature as much as possible.

I want to be spontaneous once more. As a child, teenager, and young adult, I was a lot more spontaneous, and this usually ended with positive results. I have told my wife that I want to bring that spontaneity back into my life again.

I am really aiming to be a human *doing* while also a human *being*. I want to live my life to the fullest and complete everything I looked at with the teacher in the Journal from The Room—that was about my life here, plus plenty more. When I read that Journal from The Room, next time, I want to know that I did all that I could and I completed another chapter of it.

I would like to continue writing books and sharing insights and information that can assist people in their lives. I have enjoyed receiving knowledge from reading books by other authors, and I would enjoy passing on any information that I can to readers.

When the time comes, and I am laying on my deathbed, I want to be able to look back and have no regrets about this human life. I aim to do everything that I want to do and achieve all that I possibly can.

The Future For Others

I cannot decide other people's future, but I hope that people who have read this book will be able to understand the glorious significance of The Room and use this insight and knowledge to benefit their own lives and the lives of others. I hope people who have lost a loved one are able to at least take some solace in knowing where their loved one has gone to. I hope that people who are afraid of dying will no longer be afraid and be able to live their life freely and fully without fear of there being a permanent end—because there really isn't.

I hope that people around the world will realize the importance of the connectivity we all have in The Room and will be able to apply it to their time on this Earth by allowing and promoting connections to others with love, compassion and acceptance instead of hate, selfishness and judgment. I hope that people will understand that, no matter how different someone seems, we are all Differently The Same.

I hope that people who read this book understand the knowledge and insights I have shared. If these are taken in the spirit in which I have written them, then this book can be a world-changer for many people and a huge promoter of positivity, hope, happiness and peace. It can help people understand that our time here on this Earth—living this human existence—is but a phase of a greater cycle, and that death is not the end, for a beautifully amazing place called The Room awaits us all.

I live in the knowledge that, regardless of what challenges are put before me, I will continue to live my life fully and openly and hope that you are able to as well. I have noticed that the younger generation is living in this way more and more, and it is nice to see. If they teach the next generation, who teaches the next generation and so on, then the pattern will continue, and long may it do so.

The future is not a result of choices among alternative paths offered by the present, but a place that is created – created first in the mind and will, created next in activity. The future is not some place we are going to, but one we are creating. The paths are not to be found, but made, and the activity of making them, changes both the maker and the destination. —Deborah James

Goals, Targets And Specified Results

In life we may set a list of what we would like to achieve. They can be big things or they can be small things, but whatever they are, if they are on the list, we want to achieve them. Sometimes this list is put on the back burner through circumstance, lack of time, or doubt. Circumstances such as having a family can delay completion of the list—if we put things off until the children are older. A lack of time in a busy life can make addressing your list seem impossible. Doubt can undermine your ability to face a particular item on your list. All of these may present themselves to you as good reasons not to get things from your list done.

Let us look at this a different way. How will you feel when you accomplish things from your list? What emotions will flow through your body on completing things from your list? How much of an achiever will you feel like for doing the things on your list? As we have looked at earlier in this book, negative emotions of lack—lack of time in this case—and doubt can take over if we let them. We can make goals and raise a family. We can have targets and have time for other things. We can set specified results and have the ability to reach them. Reaching your goals will really allow the positive energy to flow into your life.

When we are in The Room, we have our goals. We achieve one of these when we are born into our human existence. When we are in The Room, we have targets. They are to continue with our journeys and help others continue theirs and support them in anyway we can, by showing compassion, acceptance and understanding to others. When we are in The Room, we have specified results in the Journal we see with the teacher, and we achieve some of these at set times in our life—for example being a toddler, teenager, adult or pensioner.

We can reach goals, targets and specified results as spirit energy, and we can do the same here on earth as human beings. Set yourself the goals, targets and specified results, and enjoy the success of achieving them and the positive energy that they afford you.

When I decided to write this book, I gave myself a goal of actually completing the book once I started it. I had targets of what chapters I wanted to include and a timescale to write it in to keep me on track. I had specified results, including what messages I wished to include in this book and which insights from The Room that I could share with you. Now all these have been achieved, I can relish in the achievement and feel proud in my accomplishment. I will definitely let the positives flow through me.

Coming Together For A Common Cause

There are many times in life when people come together for a common cause: support rallies, sport or music events, charity walks and fundraisers, or merely to support a friend in need. I have an example of my own from an event that I helped organize back in the late eighties.

Radio One, a national radio station in the UK, was looking for pubs all around the country to host quiz nights in. The quiz nights were a fundraiser for the charity Children In Need. At the time, my local pub was the Beachy Head

Pub in Eastbourne. I put it forward to the radio station, and it was chosen as one of the pubs. I helped organize teams to participate, raffle prizes, run fundraising events like head shaves and promote the event to get a good crowd. The bigger the crowd, the more money we could help to raise for the charity. The evening came, and a lot of fun was had by all, a lot of hair and beards were shaved, a lot of questions answered in the quizzes, and a lot of money was raised for the cause. In this instance, there was an idea of a pub quiz and a suggestion of a pub to hold a quiz night. Me and other people ran with it and made it a possibility, until a result occurred that presented a good amount of money raised for the cause, the chosen charity. This is just one of several times that I can think off where coming together for a common cause had positive results.

The reason I have put this in here is that, when we are in The Room, we are all together, all connected, and we all work together for the common cause. We recognize that we are all on a specific level in our journey and that we all support each other in that. We can do this in The Room as spirit energy and here on Earth as human beings. If we can all come together for the common cause we can reconnect everyone and promote peace and positivity.

It Is Never Too Late For Change

This is an interesting aspect of our thinking that I have heard quite a lot in my counselling sessions, out in society as a whole, and within my own brain. Many people, including myself, have a certain idea about how life is. There are averages and majorities, and we seem to take this a being the absolute truth. Yet how many times have we seen instances shown to us of it not being too late for change? When we see this, we go, *wow,* and are in awe of the person who has made the change. This can be because we think we are too old, yet look how much longer professional athletes are lasting in their specific sports, longer than when I was a kid watching sports. I can remember as a child that I knew less than a handful of people who were relatives or friends of my family who did not smoke; indeed I even graduated into this smoking phenomenon. Yet today it is the opposite, and I probably know less than a handful of people who do smoke. That change has happened with a large number of people in a relatively short time. I see some of my friends who are my age or a bit older, and they have started running or going to the gym or competing in sports, yet the theory going around in our minds is that we are too old for change.

I know, from my own personal experience, that I was very much into this belief. When I left school with few academic grades, as far I was concerned that was that—I'd already had my chance at education. When I was working in construction and running my own landscaping business my thoughts were that this is what I would be doing until I retire—my opportunities at other occupations had passed me by. When I dislocated my shoulder and could no longer do sliding tackles in soccer, I thought that my sports career and keeping fit regime was over. Yet I have slowly overcome these.

For a long while I didn't participate in any sports or fitness programs. I worked hard physically, but felt that I could not be at my best playing sports, or even undertake other sports due to my shoulder injury. I swapped the self-pity part of my blockage for change, and I did continue to play soccer for a few seasons. Now my wife and I do exercise programs at home together, and we enjoy hiking. This is a definite change for the better.

When I decided to return to college and complete my counselling diploma, I was nervous but decided that a change was needed in my thought patterns to complete it. I visualized myself holding my diploma, even though it would still be three years before I completed it, and believe it or not, I really enjoyed learning. This also came as a major surprise to me after my years of playing truant from school!

Having the opportunity to change career was both a big step and a big change for me. I took a position as a volunteer first to see if it was a job that I really wanted to do, and once I knew that it was, I could concentrate on finding employment in that field. I remember the excitement and enthusiasm I had at being successful in getting both voluntary and paid positions. A few years before, I had thought it would never be possible, but here I was, a few years later, with a different thought-pattern, sitting in my office as a paid worker on the first day of my new career!

These are just three changes that I have had in my life where I may have thought that it would be impossible, or that change could never happen—in some cases even having *other* people telling me that nothing would change. Well I did change, and I changed what I wanted to change. I changed myself and my thought-patterns, and I will do the same in the future for any changes that I feel will benefit me or others.

I would like to give another example of changing to try and instill the message more deeply. Imagine that you have lived in the same house for the last thirty years. Imagine further that you started work at the company that you still work for on the day you moved into your house. Every day for the past thirty years you have driven north ten miles for work and ten miles back again at the end of each working day. Now, completely out of the blue, your company tells everyone that they are moving to a new building that is ten miles south of where you live. All of a sudden you have to make a change. You may have told people that you would never change, but suddenly this news has been put upon you, and if you do not agree to continue working in their new building you will be out of a job. So you agree to change and everything works out perfectly with no problems. Just think about this: even if you had said you would not go and work in their new building, you would still have had change thrust upon you by either having to find a new job or being unemployed—change would have been inevitable. If you could have changed for this situation then it shows that you can change, regardless of any denials or barriers to change that you may have put up. Change will happen at different times in our lives, so realizing that it is never too late to change offers a smooth transition to these denials and barriers. Be aware of areas that you can change for the better and acknowledge the change.

Whatever it is you think you cannot do, regardless how difficult it will be, barriers notwithstanding, please remember that change is possible. We all changed when we came from our Prior Life to this human life, and we will all change when we return to The Room. Embrace your changes.

> *It is not the strongest of the species that survives, nor the most intelligent that survives. It is the one that is the most adaptable to change.* —Charles Darwin

Enlightenment

Change and enlightenment often go hand in hand. Enlightenment occurs when you read, see, hear, taste or feel something that strikes a chord with you and you take it on as part of your belief system. Enlightenment can also be spoken—you then voice this new belief or understanding to other people. There have been—and will be—many enlightenment moments in your lives, and you will take on a percentage of these messages, views or visions to enhance your own life and also spread them out to others with the hope of enhancing their lives too. I hope that the message in this book becomes part of your enlightenment and that you will take it on and spread the word.

> *Everyone has a spirit that can be refined, a body that can be trained in some manner, a suitable path to follow. You are here to realize your inner divinity and manifest your innate enlightenment.* —Morihei Ueshiba

Learning All The Time

We never stop learning, and it is that pure and simple. Some people think that we only learn in a place of learning like school, college or university, but the whole world is our classroom. Just think about how many electrical items you have had to learn to work over the years as things progress. You have learnt to work televisions, video players, stereo music systems, DVD players, computers, MP3 players, iPads, cellphones and the list goes on. That does not include new gadgets for the home, car or workplace that will keep being developed. So as you can see with this simple list of everyday items, we are always learning. It is never too late to learn, and only we decide what we want to learn and not learn.

If we can learn how to work things this easily, we can learn how to do other things just as easily. We can learn about sports interests. We can learn about cooking. We can learn about different people and their culture, customs and traditions. You see, learning can happen all the time if we want it to, and about any subject that we choose. I grew up in the UK and did not know much about First Nations people, but over time I have learnt about their history and culture as I have an interest in it and a need to learn. It is also the same with Hawaiian people, where I have learnt a little about their culture and traditions after enjoying vacations in Hawaii. Whatever we choose to learn about we can. It is never too late, and there is always an opportunity to learn about anything, particularly with the internet being available so widely nowadays.

We left The Room to learn as human beings as part of our journey, so learning is okay to do regardless of what others may say. If you do not understand how to use your cellphone you learn how to do it, and then things that you may have been struggling with on your cellphone before become easier to understand. You can now text or take photos or add contacts to your phone, whatever it was you did not know how to do, all through taking the time to learn. If you do not understand the culture or traditions of other people take the time to learn. Enjoy having the knowledge and open up your heart to acceptance and connecting.

People Watching

Have you ever just sat in a café, looking out of the window while drinking your tea or coffee and watched people go by on the busy street outside? I have, and I quite enjoy doing it. People-watching can enable you to witness how people may scurry along if they are rushing from one work place to another, or you may see people casually walking along with all the time in the world if they are on vacation. Watching people in their everyday life is not being nosey or intrusive as they are already walking along from point A to point B—but it can be interesting to see when thinking about the human race. We were encouraged to people-watch on my counselling course and in a sociology course I took.

The reason that I am putting it in this book is this: that no matter how many times you people-watch, no matter how many people you see when people-watching and no matter how many different venues you may people-watch from, one thing remains the same. We are all Differently The Same.

Some people may be rushing around, some people may be walking at a more relaxed pace, some people may be from a different cultural group, some people may be older, some people may be younger, some people may be this or may be that or may be whatever. At the end of the day, when you people-watch, you can realize common themes; they are all human beings, they all have a human body, and they all have a spirit energy inside them that came from The Room and will return to it one day. No matter what you see while you are people-watching, make sure you remember a very important lesson from this book, we are all Differently The Same.

Go With The Flow

This is as simple as it sounds. Sometimes our lives can become quite complicated. We may have to fit in work, children, school, clubs, social times, hobbies, etc. —and *still* find time to sleep! I think sometimes we make it harder than it needs to be, and this section is a quick and easy reminder for us all. As I said, sometimes I think we make things harder because that is how it has always been or how we expected it to be.

When things run smoothly, we can sabotage it in some way to make it harder again. Instead of doing this, try to allow the flow to continue. When we are in The Room, we go with the flow and everything works in a great space–time continuum. Sometimes we need to do the same here on Earth for the benefit of ourselves. There is an album by the rock group Oasis called *(What's The Story) Morning Glory?* Well, we all have a story to tell, and this one is mine. I have gone with the flow and told it here, and I am very pleased to have done so. I could not have said that just one year ago, but now I have gone with the flow, and I am happy that I chose to.

To move forward simply set your intentions, be grateful for what you have, be open to what is possible, and the rest just happens as a beautiful and effortless flow. —Bryant McGill

Follow The Signs

We can quite often see signs that pop up in front of us. They can come in the form of suddenly seeing somebody that we may have thought about or needed to see. Or an unsolicited bit of mail showing up, a brochure with the details of a trip that you have always wanted to take—and on sale at that. There could be a job that is suddenly advertised at a place that you have always wanted to work just as you are being laid off at your current job. These are all signs, although when you pick up on them you may call them coincidences. There is nothing coincidental about them; they are all happening at the time in the flow of your life that you set in The Room.

I have an example that I will share with you here. Around four years ago I was looking for a book for my wife's birthday. I was browsing the shelves in our local bookstore when all of a sudden a book fell down from a shelf—about head height and to the right of where I was standing. There was no one standing there and I had not looked at any of those books. The lady working in the book store asked if everything was all right, and I said that all was fine and that this book had just fallen off and that I would pick it up and put it back. I bent down and picked up the book, and when I turned it around and saw the title, I noticed the book was called *The Law Of Attraction* by Esther and Jerry Hicks. I laughed out loud at this and told the lady in the shop about it, and said that I would buy that book based on the title and the way it fell on the floor, as if to get my attention. I bought the book and took it home. I wrapped it and gave it to my wife on her birthday and told her the story behind me buying it. She read the book and was so amazed by it that she asked me to read it. I read it and we discussed the contents and how it can be very useful for us to put the Law of Attraction in place in our lives, and we have. Since then we have bought more of Esther and Jerry Hicks' books and realize the power of using the Law of Attraction. All of this because I took note of a sign—not a coincidence but an out there sign—to buy a book that would be beneficial in our lives.

I have learnt to look for signs that may show up for me from time to time and accept the benefit of these freely. I believe that, with the natural flow of our journeys, these signs are aiming us towards the life that we chose from the Journal in The Room. When you see the signs, try and act on them, and reap the rewards that are on offer to you.

Heaven

One thing that strikes me is that many religions talk about a place where we will all return to—Heaven. When I think about The Room, I feel that it is possibly the heaven that it is mentioned in religion. Regardless of what differences people may have as human beings here on this Earth, it is pleasing to know that the basis of Heaven is a shared concept and that, no matter how disconnected we may have been or feel here, when we return to The Room we will have a complete connection once more. I sincerely hope this book helps to change some people's thoughts and opinions about other people so that they may change and be more allowing, accepting, and inclusive before the end of their human lives. When we return to The Room we definitely will be.

In Spirit

For me, it does not matter how you get the message, so long as you understand the message, that is what's important. Being in spirit is how some people envision us being after this human life, and from my memories of being in The Room, I can say that is how it will be; we will return to The Room as spirit energy, as a soul—in spirit if you like. In spirit forms the basis of other words or phrases and these include inspire, inspired, inspiration, inspiring, spiritual and spirit energy. As you can see, I have used a lot of these in this book and use some of them in everyday life when talking about people, animals, teams, whatever it is you want to use them with. When we are spirit energy, we are in spirit, and when we are in spirit, we are spirit energy. However you look at it, we are in The Room having a Prior Life experience. At the end of this life, we will return to The Room and be spirit energy in spirit.

The Reasons For The Chapters In This Book

When I was thinking about writing this book and putting down sample chapters, I knew the messages that I wanted to pass along, and I knew the experiences that I wanted to write about. Choosing the right chapters is very important, and I would like to tell you how and why I chose the chapters I have written in this book.

I chose to write the chapter Growing Up because I wanted to give you an insight into who I was and who I have become; a full vision of who I am. I also wanted you to experience how it felt for you to read and see this information about me, without knowing about my memory, as this is how everyone I have ever met in this world has seen me up until this year. Remember, I had not told a single person about my memory until earlier this year, when I told my wife. I wanted you to know how it will feel for my family and friends, who I have not told, when they read this. Understanding this will help you to know how you accept both my Prior Life experience and me as a person. How you process the in-The-Room knowledge that I have written about will have a result of either accepting me or not accepting me. Whatever the results—acceptance or not—the experiences I have written about, will enable you to see how you may or may not accept other people in your lives. I hope that you take it to heart and accept people with a positive perspective.

The next chapter I chose to write about is pretty self explanatory and is called So What Is My Memory? When I wrote this I realized that this would be the first time that you will have my Prior Life experience open up to you in your life. From that moment on you would either have put the book down and read something else or carry on reading, wanting to learn more about it and being open to the experience. The fact that you are now reading this sentence means that you are an open-minded person. I hope that you have enjoyed reading about my time in The Room, and I hope that you have learnt something to take away with you. I also hope that you may put some of the Prior Life experiences from The Room into your life and allow the positivity to flow with and through you and onwards into other people.

I chose to write the chapter called Valuable Lessons From The Room to share with you and the world, all the quality learning that my Prior Life experience has brought forth to me. These lessons have been with me my whole life, but I have not always set them in motion. Now I am accepting of my Prior Life experience and no longer feel the need to shut it down or try and hide it; I have begun to find an inner peace and now fully accept what I have learnt from The Room as the gift it is. This gift has been with me since day one, and now this gift has been unwrapped, taken out of the box, and shared with the whole world. These are valuable lessons that we can all take to heart. If we do our own homework with them, we can use them to benefit both our lives and the lives of other people in a positive way.

The next chapter is entitled We Are All Differently The Same. Earlier on in the book, I wrote about why I had chosen this as the name of this book, but I also wanted to expand on that as it is a very important message that I am trying to put out there, and giving this message its own chapter made perfect sense. We may look different, sound different, act differently, have differences, like different things, eat different foods and so on and so forth, but at the end of the day, we are all spirit energy that has come from The Room. We have come to Earth to participate in this working holiday as human beings, before returning as spirit energy back to The Room at the end of this human existence. Regardless of any perceived differences we are all the same—Differently The Same. When we fully accept this, we can move on and fully accept everybody, for an inclusive, connected world. This is exactly how it is in The Room, and we can replicate that beautiful scenario and way of living here on Earth. We are all Differently The Same.

I chose the next chapter Living As A Whole Person to show that we all have parts of the masculine and feminine sides within us, whether we are male or female, and it is okay to show them and use these for our own benefit. So many times in life we are told that we should be this way or that way, but we can be anyway we want to be. With male and female roles this can intensify the societal view, and this should not be so. If we are happy and doing what makes us happy that is what should be important, not a passed-down judgment from yesteryear. Allow yourself to be a whole person, and allow the whole person to be you. Live your life to the fullest, and live it as a whole person.

I chose to include this chapter called Intuitiveness because intuition has always had quite a strong connection with me. I can remember communicating intuitively in The Room, and I have included the sub-sections talking about my intuitive connections with pets, wild animals, and insects. Nature has always been important to me, and I am pleased to have been able to share theses experiences with you. I have also had intuitive times in my life, and through sharing the examples of listening to intuition and not listening to intuition, I hope that you are able to take this to heart and use intuition in your life. Intuition is something that we all had in The Room, and if we can find the intuition and use it here in our human existence then it will be of a positive for us.

The next chapter that I chose to write about is called The Law Of Attraction. The Law of Attraction is something that we can all choose to use in our lives. It is an amazing tool for manifesting our desires. When you think of something that you want to have in your life, release your rockets of desire out into the Universe, allow the manifestation to happen and come to you, and you can reap and share the results. What could be a better way to live for both yourself and others? You can manifest things into your life and other people's lives. The Law of Attraction is something that we can all use and when we eliminate doubt from our thinking. We can look forward to the positive results to come.

I chose the next chapter to give you an answer to the question Why Did I Write This Book Now? The memory that I have inside my head has been with me forever, but I have never felt comfortable sharing it for a variety of reasons. Now, after sharing my memory with my wife, children and a couple of friends, I feel good being able to pass on this knowledge. I hope that the Prior Life experiences in The Room that I have written about will be able to help those of you who have lost a loved one and those who may be afraid of dying. I also hope that the message of the book, namely that we are all Differently The Same—and spiritually connected—gets through to people so that it can be shared with others, and so that the world can be a more accepting and peaceful place for us to live and enjoy in our human existence.

I chose the next chapter A Few Things I Have Learnt Over The Years In This Human Existence, because I wanted to show a few examples of how some positive emotions and actions are with us in The Room and here on Earth, but others only exist in our human existence. I want to show

how using certain emotions and actions in our lives can enhance our time here on Earth—both for us and other people around us—and how using other negative emotions can be of a detriment to us. Using the examples that I included in this chapter, I hope that you can see that we do have a choice in what we do and that the better the choice, the better our life is. Why choose a stale slice of bread when you can choose a fresh slice? Choose positive emotions and actions in your life.

I wrote the next chapter The Importance Of It All because I really want to reiterate the importance of the messages in this book. I would like you to look at it this way. Imagine there is an engine stripped down and all the individual parts are lying on the workshop floor. You may know what certain parts are and what they do, but may not fully comprehend how they all work together to make the engine run. That is the same with this book. I truly want to emphasize the importance of the insights and knowledge that my Prior Life experiences in The Room mean and how we can use them to enhance our lives on this Earth as human beings.

The final chapter is called In Conclusion. I chose to write this chapter because I wanted to show where I want to take my life and the road on which I will continue to travel. I want to show what I see other people are capable of bringing into their future and how it may be of benefit to them. I also want to show that change can happen at any time and it is never too late. We have changed over the years; we have been alive, and we have chosen those changes. We can change over the years that we have left as human beings and choose what changes we want to make. We all have the choices for our own future; choose wisely and positively.

There are lots of sub-headers that I have used in this book, and there is a specific reason for each one. I decided to split them into sub-headers so that they will be easier to find if you would like to revisit certain chapters or sub-headers for future reading. Each sub-header has a strong message behind it and has a powerful connection to the chapter in which it's found. I feel that each sub-header has something important to give, and I did not want to hide the information in long, wordy paragraphs. The messages they have can be useful for you in your human life. I have enjoyed writing every single word in this book, and I hope that you have enjoyed reading it as much.

I have added a few different quotes where they fit nicely together with the written message. I wrote them so that they may also be able to reinforce exactly what I am trying to convey to you in the corresponding chapter and in this book.

The reason that I have added this specific subsection is that I wanted to repeat and confirm to you all one last time everything that is in this book, why it is there and how I feel it can be of benefit to you and other people. Repetition can allow greater learning, and I truly hope that you have been able to learn and understand the messages that I have passed on here and that you will be able to accept and use them in your own lives and with other people. The reason for this book is that I hope it may be of benefit to the world.

Find The Courage

When I was younger writing this book would have been impossible. Even last year, I would not have been able to write it, but this year I conquered some fears. First of all I told my wife all about my memory and opened up my Prior Life experience in The Room to the first person ever. Secondly, after deliberating about it for a few months, I have put all of my experiences, insights, learning, knowledge and understanding from my Prior Life down in writing in this book. By doing so, I am sharing all this information with the world to offer everyone the possibility of benefiting from my memory. Thirdly, I do not care what people may think about what I have written, even if they only offer comments from a negative perspective. I KNOW my experience, and nothing can take that away from me. Sometimes I think people can become afraid of books like this through a lack of under-standing and can see anything like this as spooky or super-natural and be almost scared of it. I have seen people roll their eyes when New Age or spiritual topics come up, even though they may have no understanding at all about any of it.

This book is not New Age; it has been with me all my forty odd years on this planet and with me longer in The Room, and when you consider that there is no space–time continuum in The Room I cannot say how old these learn-ings are.

I do not know why I have these memories. Perhaps we all do and then forget them—but for whatever reason I didn't; they stayed installed in my brain. What I do know is that they are there—and now they are here in this book. I have found the courage to write this book, and I hope that you are able to find the courage to learn from anything in it that may benefit you. Now I have broken through with this act of courage. I aim to conquer some more personal battles and have constant improvement, learning and happiness in my life.

And the day came when the risk to remain tight in a bud was more painful than the risk it took to blossom. —Anaïs Nin

Putting It On The Line

When I wrote this book I knew that I would be opening up certain aspects of my life publicly. I also knew that opening up these aspects can be rewarded with positive feedback or ridiculed with negativity. Looking through the chapters and sub-headers in this book I had to decide what I wanted to leave in and what I wanted to leave out. I decided to leave it all in and put it on the line. Talking about my Prior Life experience is becoming a lot more natural for me now and I am willing to talk about it in further detail with people who are interested in it. When I looked back at what I had included in the book the only section I had to really think hard about leaving in was the intuitiveness with wild animals and insects sections. After a lot of thinking I made the decision to leave them in because I want to show the full aspect of my Prior Life experience and intuitiveness was one of them. I feel that putting it in writing about how I have had these intuitive situations can enable us to realise that we can expand our intuitiveness and gain positives from it. It also shows the connection that everything here on Earth has, as we sometimes seem to think that as humans we are the only ones here with thoughts and feelings. Everything that I have included in this book I am comfortable sharing otherwise it would not have been included in here. I am happy to put it on the line to help enhance and spread the message that we are all differently the same.

Final Thoughts

I am not an angel, and I have not lived a perfect life. Even with my Prior Life knowledge, I chose to live my life with my decisions, whether right or wrong. I can admit my mistakes, and I can and will learn from them. I will focus on living my life the best way that I can in the future. I have become more and more spiritual over the years, and moving to Canada has enhanced that for me, both with the people and the nature here. So long as I can remember my in-The-Room experiences and put them to positive use, I will be happy with my life, knowing I will be doing the best for me and others. If, after reading this book, you are able to do the same, then this book has been written both for a common purpose and a successful result.

I have written this book with the purpose of sharing my Prior Life experiences and my in The Room memories to help people understand that there is more to living than just life itself. It took a long time for me to muster the courage to tell anyone about my memory, and it took me a little longer to pluck up enough courage to put it all down in words. I have enjoyed writing and sharing this with you, and I hope that you are able to take it in the spirit in which it was intended.

I can only write about what I know, so everything that is here is from a knowing point of view. There may be questions that are not answered here, and I hope that more answers and memories will come back to me now that I am open to them again. I have only written about I know, and have refused to be drawn into speculation. As much as I would like to rekindle my memories and bring them back down from the shelf unto which they were packed many years ago, I will only share memories once they come back to me.

I have avoided reading certain books and have avoided hypnosis, as I wanted this book to be written from my natural memory. I will now read those books—after all it was because of a book that helped me tell my memory in the first place—and one day I may decide to try hypnosis to see if my memories can be accessed this way. Who knows?

What I do know is that writing this book has meant a lot to me and enabled me to get something out in the open that has been with me for a very long time. It is a positive thing to pass on, and I am very happy sharing it with you.

P. S. Just One More Thing

I had originally finished this manuscript and spoken to the publishers regarding getting the book printed, but I just wanted to add this last sub-section. The day after meeting with the publisher, I went to the movie theatre and saw *Cloud Atlas*. If you have not seen it, I do not want to give anything away and ruin it for you, but near the end there is a scene where one of the main characters is being interrogated about something, and she is asked why she decided to tell her story and make it public. Her response was along the lines of *because I wanted to get my message across before I died and my message lost forever.* She is then asked, *what if nobody believes you*, to which she replies, *someone already has!*

This is true of me and my situation and the memory that I have carried around with me my whole life. Before writing this book I told a small handful of people about my memory and they believed me. They were interested in my memory and experiences in The Room and what I had to say about it. I hope that you are too and that you are able to take away some information or knowledge that may be helpful to you or someone you know. Thank you for reading this book, and please remember that we are all Differently The Same.

Until next time.